LIBRARY OF CONGRESS

Geography and Maps

AN ILLUSTRATED GUIDE

LIBRARY OF CONGRESS WASHINGTON 1996

This publication was made possible by generous support from the James Madison
Council, a national, private-sector advisory council dedicated to helping the Library of
Congress share its unique resources with the nation and the world.

Geography and Maps is composed in Centaur, a typeface designed by American typography
and book designer Bruce Rogers (1870–1957). The full type font was first used at the
Montague Press in 1915 for an edition of Maurice de Guérin's *The Centaur*.

This guide was compiled by Ralph E. Ehrenberg, Gary L. Fitzpatrick, James A. Flat-
ness, Ronald E. Grim, and Richard W. Stephenson, with the assistance of Michael
Buscher, Kathryn Engstrom, Charlotte Houtz, Robert Locke, Robert Morris, Edward
Redmond, and Patricia Van Ee. It was edited by Iris Newsom, Publishing Office, and
designed by Robert Wiser, Archetype Press, Inc., Washington, D.C.

COVER: Henricus Hondius' world map, first published in 1633. See full illustration on
pages 10 and 11.

LIBRARY OF CONGRESS CATALOGING-IN-PUBLICATION DATA

Library of Congress. Geography and Map Division.
    Library of Congress geography and maps : an illustrated guide / [compiled
by Ralph E. Ehrenberg. . . . et al.].
        p.   cm.
    ISBN 0–8444–0817–4
    ————— ———— Copy 3. Z663.35 .L44   1996
    1. Maps — Bibliography — Catalogs. 2. Atlases — Bibliography — Cat-
alogs. 3. Remote sensing — Bibliography — Catalogs. 4. Library of Congress.
Geography and Map Division — Catalogs. I. Ehrenberg, Ralph E., 1937–.
II. Title. III. Title : Geography and maps.
    Z6028.L52 1996
    [GA195.W374]
    912′.074753—dc20

94–20385
CIP

For sale by the U.S. Government Printing Office
Superintendent of Documents
P.O. Box 371954
Pittsburgh, PA 15250–7954

Contents

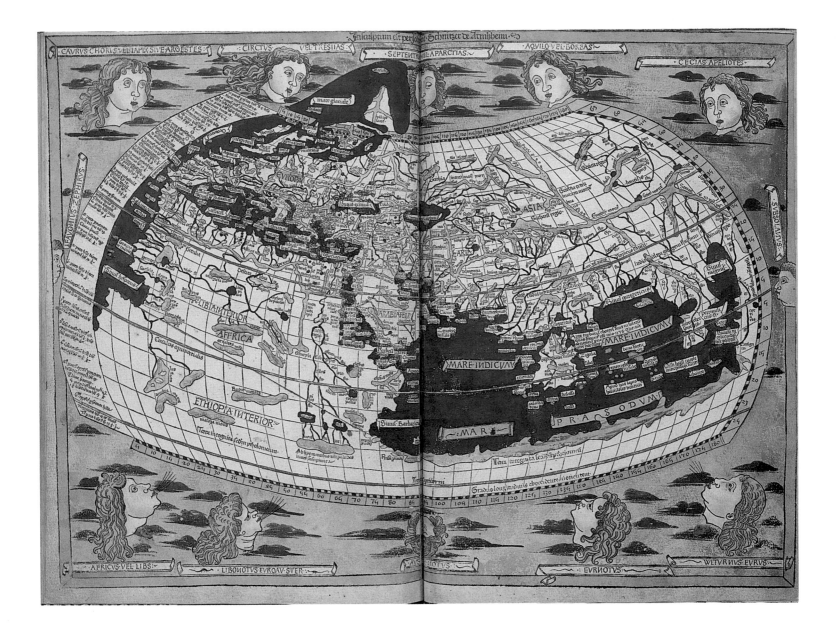

Introduction

MAPS AND ATLASES have been an important part of the collections of the Library of Congress since its beginning in 1800 when a joint congressional committee purchased three maps and an atlas from a London dealer. From this modest beginning, the Library's cartographic holdings have grown during the past two centuries to more than 4,250,000 map sheets, 53,000 atlases, 700,000 microfilm images, 300 globes, 2,000 terrain models, 1,600,000 aerial photographs and remote sensing images, and 1,820 computer files.

The Geography and Map Division has custody of the bulk of the Library's cartographic materials. Established in 1897 as the Hall of Maps to serve Congress and federal agencies, the Geography and Map Division today functions as the National Map Library. Its primary responsibility is developing the Library's cartographic collections. An average of some seventy thousand items are acquired yearly through government deposits, transfers of superceded maps from federal libraries, copyright deposits, domestic and international exchanges, purchases, and gifts. These range from rare atlases to state-of-the-art electronic maps, but the major focus of the Geography and Map Division acquisition program is acquiring current materials from all countries. While many of the current items are acquired through exchanges and deposits, the division relies heavily on public-spirited citizens to assist in the acquisition of rare maps and unique collections. The cartographic collections date from the fourteenth century and cover virtually every country and subject.

The Geography and Map Division serves as a major center for scholarly research relating to cartography and geography. Linking the scholar and the collection is an experienced staff of reference librarians and senior specialists. Reference activities are centered in the Geography and Map Division Reading Room, located in room LM-B01, on the basement level of the James Madison Memorial Building. The reference facilities consist of a map and atlas reading room, with a seating capacity for thirty-two, a microform reading area, and a Geographic Information Systems reference facility.

An essential element of the Geography and Map Division's effort to link the scholar and collection is the publication of finding aids that direct researchers to individual items. Since its establishment, the division has published almost fifty cartobibliographies devoted to specific geographic areas, special formats, individual collections, and specific subjects. Scholarly access to the cartographic collections is enhanced by the preparation of map exhibitions and the sponsorship of professional meetings and conferences such as the International Map Collector's Society (IMCOS) and the Washington Map Society.

Take a map and travel.

CLARA EGLI LEGEAR
On the occasion of celebrating seventy-five years of service to the Library of Congress as map librarian and volunteer, 1989.

OPPOSITE: A map of the classical image of the world from the 1482 edition of Claudius Ptolemy's *Geographia* which was printed in Ulm, Germany, by Lienhart Holle. Derived from a manuscript copy prepared by the Benedictine monk Donnus Nicolaus Germanus who worked in Florence, Italy, from 1460 to 1482, it is the first atlas printed north of the Alps and the first one to contain maps printed from woodblocks. (*Atlas Collection*)

Maps acquired by the division since 1969 have been cataloged, and their bibliographic records are available through the Library's MARC (Machine Readable Cataloging) Maps database which is available in most libraries through national networks. This database is also available on microfilm. As a major service to the map library community, the Division establishes, maintains, and disseminates national standards for classifying and cataloging maps and atlases through the MARC Map system.

The Division also facilitates linkages between researchers and the vast resources of geographic data available in the nation's capital. Because it is located in Washington, D.C., the center of the mapping and remote sensing industry in the United States, the Division has evolved as a national cartographic and geographic information and referral center.

In 1901, Philip Lee Phillips, the first chief of the Hall of Maps, reported to the Librarian of Congress that: "This collection, which is the largest extant, will in time be of great value, not only to the cartographer, but also to the historian." Due to the tireless efforts of Phillips and five generations of map librarians, the Geography and Map Division's collection of cartographic materials is of even greater value today . In addition to cartographers, geographers, and historians, the collection is heavily used by genealogists, preservationists, urban planners, ecologists, and scientists.

In an effort to reach a wider audience and to further develop, enhance, and promote the Library's geographic and cartographic collections, the Geography and Map Division established in 1995 two support groups: the Philip Lee Phillips Society, an association of friends of the Division, and the Center for Geographic Information, a partnership of private sector firms and the Division.

RALPH E. EHRENBERG, CHIEF
GEOGRAPHY AND MAP DIVISION

Detail from Antoine Lafréry's rare 1572 copperplate engraving of Olaus Magnus's map of Scandinavia and the North Atlantic, first published in Venice in 1539. Magnus was a Swedish ecclesiastic and humanist who drew this map to show the northern lands lost to the Catholic faith through the Reformation. (*Atlas Collection*)

Buda and Pest, the two ancient Hungarian cities divided by the Danube River, are depicted on this view, which is typical of the city views and plans contained in Georg Braun and Franz Hogenberg's great work, *Civitates Orbis Terrarum*. Published in Cologne in six volumes during the years 1572 to 1618, this work is considered the first systematic city atlas ever published. *(Atlas Collection)*

Atlases

A scholar who never travels but stays at home is not worthy to be accounted a scholar. From my youth on I had the ambition to travel, but could not afford to wander over the three hundred counties of Korea, much less the whole world. So, carrying out an ancient practise, I drew a geographical atlas. And while gazing at it for long stretches at a time I feel as though I was carrying out my ambition … Morning and evening while bending over my small study table, I meditate on it and play with it — and there in one vast panorama are the districts, the prefectures and the four seas, and endless stretches of thousands of miles.

WON HAK-SAENG
KOREAN STUDENT
Preface to his untitled manuscript atlas of China during the Ming Dynasty, dated 1721.

OPPOSITE: The voyages of Christopher Columbus, John Cabot, and Amerigo Vespucci dramatically changed the world map. One of the earliest printed maps to incorporate this new world view was Johann Ruysch's map which is found in the 1507 reprinting of the 1490 Rome edition of Ptolemy's *Geographia*, both of which are represented in the division. It is believed that Ruysch, a native of Antwerp, accompanied Bristol seamen on a voyage to the great fishing banks off the coast of Newfoundland in about 1500. (*Atlas Collection*)

THE GEOGRAPHY AND MAP DIVISION holds more than 53,000 atlases, the largest and most comprehensive collection in the world. Additional rare atlases are found in the Rare Book and Special Collections Division. Geographical coverage of the atlas collection is heavily weighted toward the United States (47 percent), world (19 percent), and Europe (16 percent). Some 20,000 atlases acquired before 1973 are described in Philip Lee Phillips and Clara Egli LeGear's *A List of Geographical Atlases in the Library of Congress with Bibliographic Notes* (9 volumes, Washington, 1909–1992) and LeGear's *United States Atlases* (2 volumes, Washington, 1950–1953). These monumental works represent a singular contribution to the field of the history of cartography by Mrs. LeGear who contributed to this project from 1914 to 1992, an unprecedented seventy-eight years (forty-two years as a staff member and thirty-six years as a volunteer).

The earliest atlases in the Library are associated with Claudius Ptolemy, an Alexandrian scholar who recorded and systematized classical Greek geographical knowledge during the second century. His *Geographia* was the first and most popular cartographic publication to be printed from movable type in the fifteenth and early sixteenth centuries. The Library holds forty-seven of the fifty-six known copies of Ptolemy's *Geographia* dating from 1475 to 1883, plus five variants and thirty-four duplicates, including rare copies of the 1482 Ulm edition, the 1490 Rome edition, the 1507 Rome edition with Johann Ruysch's world map incorporating the exploration of the New World by John Cabot, and the 1513 Strassburg edition with twenty supplemental maps including two new maps showing America.

A prized atlas treasure is a bound collection of maps assembled by Antoine Lafréry, a native of Burgundy who moved to Rome about 1540 and set up shop as an engraver and publisher. During this time the European map trade was dominated by cartographers in Rome and Venice who had perfected copperplate engraving for maps. Lafréry and other Italian publishers and dealers began to assemble these individual maps into bound folio volumes based on the interests of their customers. About seventy of these composite Italian atlases are extant today, each unique in its contents. In 1943, the Library purchased nine additional map sheets that were at one time part of a Lafréry atlas.

Abraham Ortelius revolutionized the map trade by publishing the first modern atlas. With the publication of his *Theatrvm orbis terrarvm* [Theater of the World] in Antwerp in 1570, the first book of maps uniform in size and design, the center of the European map trade shifted from Rome and Venice to Antwerp, the largest and most active port city in Europe. Engraved mainly by Franz Hogenberg and printed by Christoffel Plantijn, the first edition consists of seventy maps

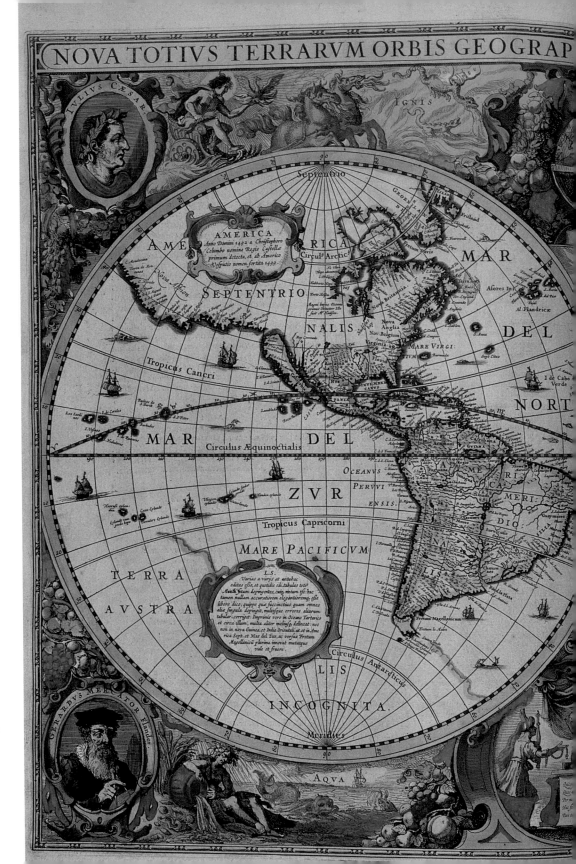

NOVA TOTIVS TERRARVM ORBIS GEOGRAP

IVLIVS CESAR

IGNIS

Septentrio

GROENL.

AMERICA
Anno Domini 1492 a Christophoro
Columbo nomine Regis Castelle
primum detecta, et ab America
Vesputio nomen sortita 1499

Ame — RICA

MAR

Frisland

Circuli Arcticus

SEPTENTRIO

Asores Inf

DEL

NALIS

Nova
Anglia
Nov. Belgium

I de Cabo
Verde

Tropicus Cancri

MARE VIRGI:
VM

Bermuda

NORT

Circulus Æquinoctialis

MAR

DEL

OCEANVS

A — ME — RI — CA

ZVR

PERVVI

MERI:

ENSIS.

DIO

Tropicus Capricorni

NA — LIS

MARE PACIFICVM

L.S.
Varias a varijs et ante hac
editas esse, et quotidie eib. tabulas tri..
Auctu fatum Longiores, cuiq; rei tum est: hac
tamen nullam accuratiorem elegantioremq; esse
libere dico; quippe que succinctius quam omnes
alie singula depingit, multisque errores aliarum
tabular. corrigit. Imprimis vero in Oceano Tartarico
et circa illum, multa aliter melius; delineat: nec
non in nova Guinea, et India Orientali, ut et in Ame
rica Sept. et Mar del Tur, ac verus Fretum
Magellanicu plurima innovit mutatque
vale et fruere.

TERRA

AVSTRA

LIS

Fretum Magellanicum

Fretum le Maire

Circulus Antarcticus

LIS

INCOGNITA.

GERARDVS MERCATOR Flander

Meridies

AQVA

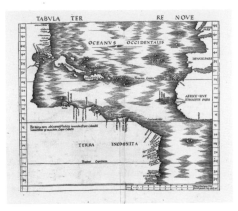

ABOVE: Martin Waldseemüller's 1513 edition of Ptolemy was a landmark work that contributed to major advances in both Renaissance geography and map printing. Published by Johann Schott in Strassburg, it depicts for the first time in an atlas format the newly discovered continents of North and South America connected by a coastline. *(Atlas Collection)*

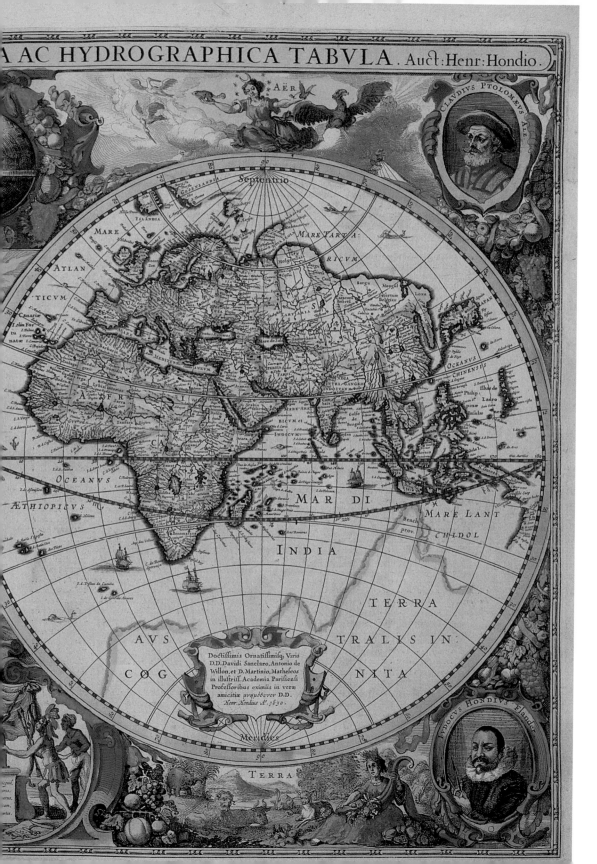

A AC HYDROGRAPHICA TABVLA. Auct: Henr: Hondio.

LEFT: Henricus Hondius's ornately decorated world map first appeared in the 1633 edition of the *Atlas* that was originally published in 1595 by the Flemish cartographer Gerard Mercator and subsequently published by Jodocus Hondius and his sons, Jodocus, Jr. and Henricus, and his son-in-law, Jan Jansson. The world is depicted in two hemispheres, which are bordered by the representation of the four elements of fire, air, water, and land as well as portraits of Julius Ceasar, the second-century (A.D.) geographer Claudius Ptolemy, and the atlas's first two publishers, Mercator and Hondius. *(Atlas Collection)*

Title page from Pieter van den Keere's *La Germanie Inférievre* (Amsterdam, 1622), the first original atlas of the Netherlands published in folio size. Strong nationalistic overtones are evident in its iconography, which is typical of the elaborately decorated title pages found in Dutch atlases of the period. *(Atlas Collection)*

on fifty-three sheets assembled from the best available sources. Extremely popular in its day, numerous editions were issued from 1570 to 1724 in Latin, Dutch, French, German, English, and Italian. The Library's collection of Orteliana is one of the largest in the world. Of the eighty-two editions identified, the Library possesses fifty-nine, a number of which are unique.

The name most associated with advancing cartography as a science during this formative period is the Flemish geographer Gerard Mercator who helped free geography from its Ptolemaic influence by his prodigious contributions in the production of globes, maps, map projections, and atlases. Through the generosity of Melville Eastham the division received copies of his magnum opus, *Atlas sive cosmographicæ meditationes de fabrica mundi et fabricati figvra* (Duisburg, 1595), and the first two parts of this atlas which were issued as separate publications prior to Mercator's death in 1594, *Galliae tabule geographicæ* (Duisburg, 1585) and *Italiae, Sclavoniæ, et Græciæ tabule geographice* (Duisburg, 1589). The Library has copies of these editions as well as representative copies of subsequent editions published by Jodocus Hondius, who purchased the plates in 1606, and by his son Henricus and Jan Jansson.

Other rare pre-1600 printed world atlases include Gerard de Jode's, *Specvlvm orbis terrarvm* [Mirror of the World] (Antwerp, 1578), one of twelve recorded copies; Christopher Saxton's *An Atlas of England and Wales* (London, 1579), the first atlas of any country, which is called "the Elizabethan atlas" because each map bears the coat of arms of Queen Elizabeth and Thomas Seckford, one of the Queen's Masters of Requests, who commissioned the maps; Corneille Wytfliet's *Descriptionis Ptolemaicæ avgmentvm, siue Occidentis* (Louvain, 1597), the first atlas devoted exclusively to the New World; Matthias Quad's *Evropae totivs orbis terrarvm* (Cologne, 1592); and Maurice Bouguereau's *Le théâtre françois* [Tours, 1594], one of nine known copies of the first national atlas of France.

The Golden Age of Dutch Cartography that was inaugurated by Ortelius and Mercator found its fullest expression during the seventeenth century with the production of monumental multivolume world atlases in Amsterdam by Joan Blaeu, Jan Jansson, Claes Janszoon Visscher, Abraham Goos, and Frederik de Wit. The division possesses excellent representative copies of all of these publishers, including Joan Blaeu's *Le grand atlas* (Amsterdam, 1667), a monumental twelve-volume French edition; Jansson's *Novus Atlas* (Amsterdam, 1658); and Joan Blaeu's Spanish edition of *Atlas mayor*, which he issued between 1659 and 1672. The Spanish edition is very rare because almost the whole edition was destroyed by fire in 1672 when the publishing house of Blaeu was burned. About twenty copies are known to exist in public libraries and private collections.

During the eighteenth century Dutch publishing houses continued the tradition of publishing voluminous atlases, often assembled from maps acquired from other firms. The Library's copy of Johannes Cóvens and Cornelis Mortier's *Atlas nouveau* (Amsterdam, 1761?) includes 922 maps bound into nine volumes while its Reiner and Josua Ottens's *Atlas maior* (Amsterdam, 1641–1729) contains 835 maps by various cartographers, all beautifully hand colored. Housed in the Rare Book and Special Collections Division is a copy of the largest atlas ever published. Issued in sixty-six volumes by Pieter van der Aa between 1700 and 1729, the *Galerie agréable du monde* contains more than three thousand plates and maps. Of the 100 sets originally printed, only a few complete copies survive today.

The center of the European map trade began to shift from the Low Countries to France in the 1650s with the publication of Nicolas Sanson's *Cartes générales de tovtes les parties dv monde* in Paris in 1654 which introduced French precision in mapping. Extremely rare in its unaltered state, the division possesses a copy of the second edition printed in 1658 and a two-volume 1670 edition with 153 maps. Among other copies of Sanson's atlases is his *Géographie universelle* (Paris, 1675?), dedicated in manuscript to the Dauphin, son of Louis XIV. Sanson was succeeded by Alexis Hubert Jaillot who was named Géographe Ordinaire du Roi in 1675. Two variant copies of his two-volume *Atlas françois* (Paris, 1695) are found in the division, one containing 123 maps, the other 138 maps.

French geographers placed cartography on a firm scientific footing during the eighteenth century, and many of their maps reflect original surveys or first-hand accounts obtained from French explorers and missionaries. The division holds a large number of French atlases from this period including works by Jean Baptiste Nolin; Guillaume Delisle, the leading cartographer of his era; Philippe Buache, a theoretical geographer; Jean Baptiste Bourguignon d'Anville; and Gilles and Didier Robert de Vaugondy, whose *Atlas universel* (Paris, 1757–1758) was published with the support of Madame de Pompadour.

British world atlases date from John Speed's *A Prospect of the Most Famous Parts of the World*, first published in London in 1627. The division possesses a copy of the 1631 edition and two variants of his *The Theatre of the Empire of Great Britain* (London, 1676), which includes a copy of *Prospect*. The division also has a copy of Moses Pitt's *English Atlas* (4 volumes, Oxford, 1680–1683), which remained incomplete when Pitt was imprisoned in the Fleet for debt. Other prolific British publishers during the end of the eighteenth and early nineteenth century for which the division holds numerous copies of their world atlases are Thomas Kitchin, Herman Moll, Robert Sayer, John Cary, Thomas Jefferys, William Faden, and John Arrowsmith.

Frontispiece from Joan Blaeu's *Le Grand Atlas*, volume 1 (Amsterdam, 1667). Issued in twelve volumes, the French edition of Blaeu's great work is one of the largest and most elaborate atlases ever produced. It contains about six hundred exquisitely engraved and colored maps, plans, and drawings of all parts of the known world. The allegorical scene, showing the figure of Geography in a chariot drawn by two lions, is based on a painting by Peter Paul Rubens. The personification of the four continents is displayed by female figures associated with appropriate animals. (*Atlas Collection*)

The division's holdings of German and Italian eighteenth-century atlases are represented by Johann Baptist Homann, geographer to Charles VI, Holy Roman Emperor, who revitalized German cartography with his *Neuer Atlas* (Nuremberg, 1730) and *Grosser Atlas* (Nuremberg, 1737), both of which were reissued numerous times; Matthaeus Seutter; Vincenzo Coronelli, an Italian globe and atlas publisher; and Franz Anton Schraembl, who published the first world atlas in Austria.

Both manuscript and printed sea atlases are well represented in the collection. The earliest sea atlases were derived during the late thirteenth century in Italy or Majorca from portolan charts which in turn had evolved from sailing guides, known as *portolanos*. Excellent examples of rare illuminated portolan atlases are found in the Vellum Chart Collection, including works by Battista Agnese (Venice, 1544); Joan Martines (Messina, circa 1560); and Jean André Brémond (Marseilles, 1670).

The Library's collection of printed sea atlases begins with Benedetto Bordone's *Libro … de tutte l'isole del mondo* (Venice, 1528), the first book of island maps. The next major advance in the development of the printed sea atlases dates from the publication of Lucas Janszoon Waghenaer's *Spieghel der zeevaerdt* [Mariners Mirror] by Christoffel Plantijn in Leyden in 1585, which contains the first charts on a common scale, a manual of practical navigation, and sailing directions for the North Atlantic off the coast of Europe. The Library possesses copies of the 1585 Dutch edition and 1586 Latin edition as well as the 1588 English edition translated by Sir Anthony Ashley.

The Dutch dominated the chart trade during the seventeenth century through the privately owned East and West India Companies, established in 1602 and 1621, respectively. Selected titles among the division holdings are listed to suggest the comprehensive nature of this material: Willem Barendsz's *Description de la mer Méditerranée* (Amsterdam, 1607), the first sea-pilot for the Mediterranean Sea; Willem Janszoon Blaeu's *The Light of Navigation* (Amsterdam, 1622); Pieter Goos's *De Zee-atlas* (Amsterdam, 1666); Joannes van Loon's *Klaer lichtende noort-ster ofte zee atlas* (Amsterdam, 1661); and Joannes van Keulen's *The Great and Newly Enlarged Sea Atlas* (3 volumes, Amsterdam, 1682–1686), an English edition of the great Dutch work.

French and British charts began to replace the hold that Dutch charts had on the atlas trade during the eighteenth century with the expansion of maritime activities in these two countries. The *Neptune françois* (Amsterdam and Paris, 1693–1700), prepared under official French auspices and published simultaneously in Paris by Jaillot and in Amsterdam by Mortier, includes some seventy

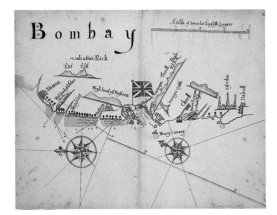

The harbor of Bombay as depicted in William Hacke's *A Description of the Sea Coasts.* Known as the "Buccaneer's Atlas," this manuscript work was compiled in London about 1690 from Spanish charts captured by the English privateer, Bartholomew Sharpe. *(Atlas Collection)*

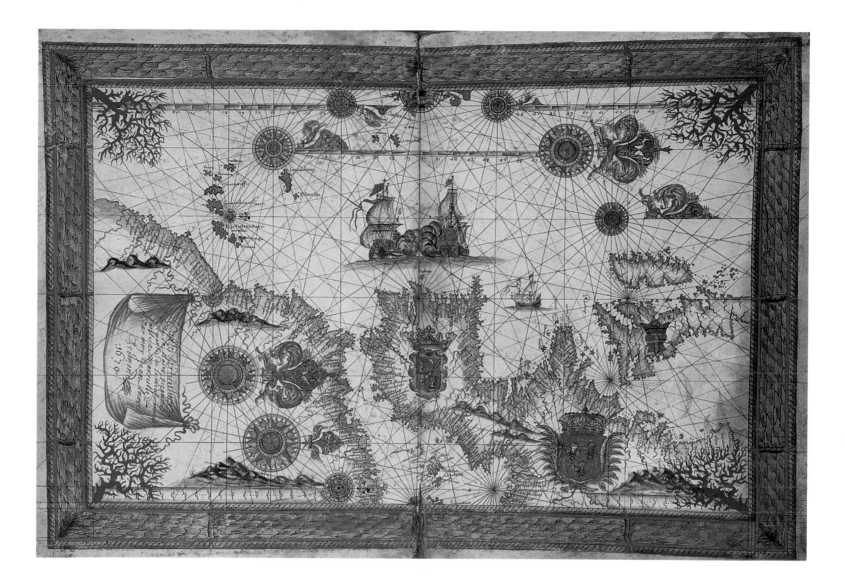

ABOVE: Chart of northwest Africa and Western Europe from Jean André Brémond's manuscript portolan atlas compiled in Marseilles in 1670. *(Vellum Chart Collection)*

SUCCESSIVE PAGES: Nautical chart of the Mediterranean Sea from *Le Neptune françois* by the artist-engraver Romein de Hooghe. Part of a two-volume work prepared initially under official French auspices but re-engraved for commercial use, it was published privately by Pieter Mortier in Amsterdam in 1693. Although the Dutch dominated the market for charts and sea atlases throughout the seventeenth century, French hydrographers were the first to place hydrographic surveying on a scientific basis. *(Atlas Collection)*

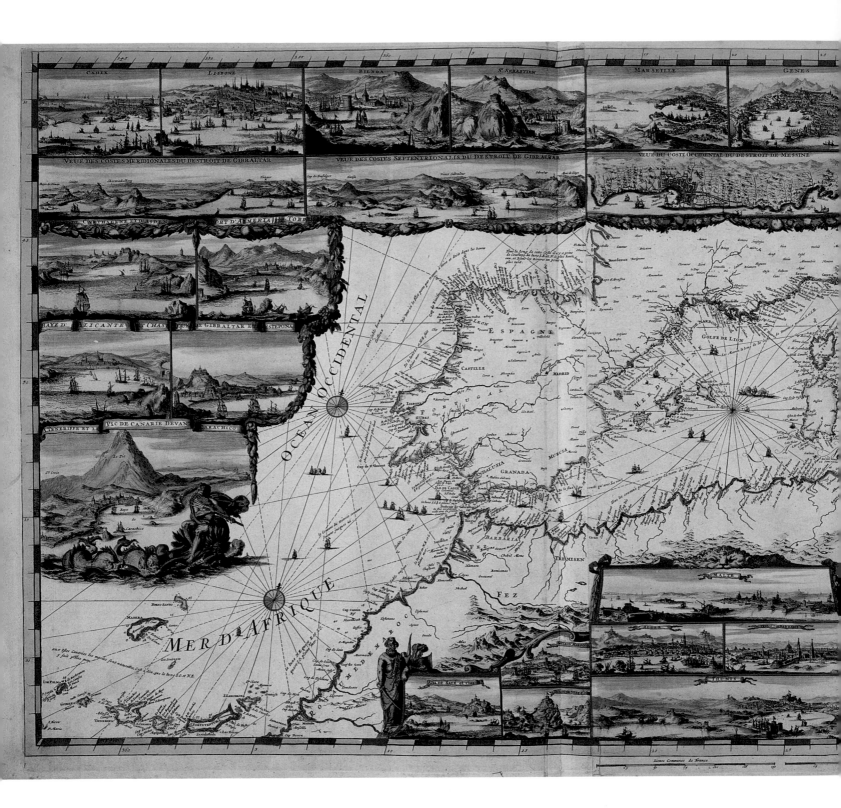

CADIX   LISBONE   BILBOA   S. SEBASTIEN   MARSEILLE   GENES

VEUE DES COSTES MERIDIONALES DU DESTROIT DE GIBRALTAR   VEUE DES COSTES SEPTENTRIONALIS DU DESTROIT DE GIBRALTAR   VEUE DU COSTE OCCIDENTAL DU DESTROIT DE MESSINE

OCEAN OCCIDENTAL

ESPAGNE

PORTUGAL

CASTILLE

MADRID

MER D'AFRIQUE

GOLFE DE LION

MER MEDITERRANE

ANDALUSIA

GRANADA

MURCIA

BARBARIA

FEZ

MAROC

MALTE

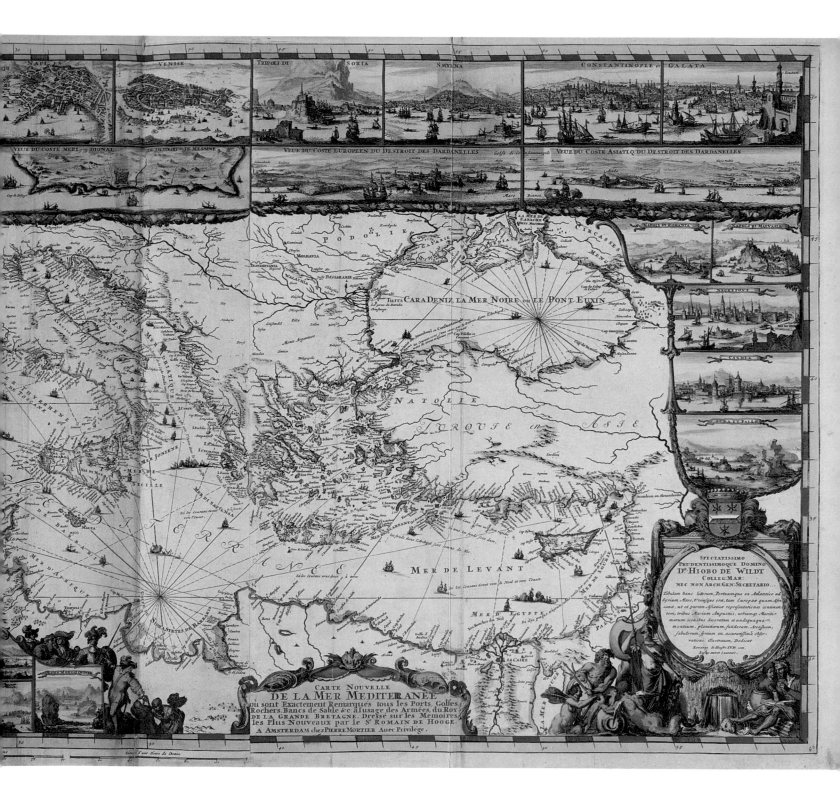

NAPLES

VENISE

TRIPOLI DI SORIA

SMYRNA

CONSTANTINOPLE et GALATA

VEUE DU COSTÉ MERIDIONAL DU DESTROIT DE MESSINE

VEUE DU COSTÉ EUROPÉEN DU DESTROIT DES DARDANELLES

VEUE DU COSTÉ ASIATIQ: DU DESTROIT DES DARDANELLES

NAPOLI DE ROMANIA

NAPOLI DI MALVASIE

NEGROPONT

CANDIA

PODOLIE

MOLDAVIA

TRANSILVANIA

WALACHIA

BESSARABIE

CRIM

TARTARIE

CIRCASSIE

MENGRELIE

Turcs CARA DENIZ la MER NOIRE ou LE PONT EUXIN

NATOLIE

TURQUIE en ASIE

MER ADRIATIQUE

MER TYRRHENE

MER JONIENE

SICILE

MER DI SAPIENSA

MER DE SCARFANTO

MER DE LEVANT

MER DE SOURIE

MER D'EGYPTE

LA MER ROUGE

SPECTATISSIMO
PRUDENTISSIMOQUE DOMINO
D[no]. HIOBO DE WILDT
COLLEG: MAR:
NEC NON ARCH: GEN: SECRETARIO...

CARTE NOUVELLE
DE LA MER MEDITERRANÉE
où sont Exactement Remarqués tous les Ports, Golfes,
Rochers, Bancs de Sable &c. a l'usage des Armées du Roy
DE LA GRANDE BRETAGNE. Dressé sur les Memoires
les Plus Nouveaux par le Sr ROMAIN DE HOOGE
A AMSTERDAM chez Pierre Mortier Avec Privilege.

Lieues d'une Heure de Chemin

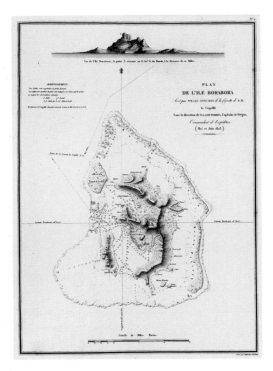

Chart of Bora Bora, French Polynesia, 1823, from Louis Isidore Duperrey's *Voyage autour du Monde ... Hydrographie, Atlas* (Paris, 1827). Duperrey led a scientific expedition around the world from 1822 to 1825. French scientific expeditions by Baudin, Freycinet, Duperrey, and Dumont d'Urville pioneered the concept of publishing the results of exploratory voyages in a series of volumes oriented to different disciplines. *(Atlas Collection)*

charts of the Atlantic and Mediterranean coasts. Jacques Nicolas Bellin's *Atlas maritime* (Paris, 1751) superceded Jaillot's atlas and continued to be issued into the nineteenth century. Early British maritime atlases are represented by Sir Robert Dudley's *Dell'arcano del mare* (Florence, 1646–1647), the first maritime atlas to use the Mercator projection and a beautiful example of the engraver's art; John Seller's rare copy of the *The English Pilot* (London, 1671), which initiated the printed chart trade in England; and four variants of Seller's *Atlas maritimus, or the sea-atlas* (London, 1675). By the turn of the nineteenth century most charts were produced as separates, but the collection includes one American sea atlas by Edmund March Blunt, the leading American chart maker. Published in 1830, it consists of fourteen charts of the Atlantic Ocean.

Complementing the seas atlases are atlases prepared to accompany the great voyages of discovery during the late eighteenth century. These include one of five known copies of Thomas Jefferys's *Collection of Charts of the Coasts of Newfoundland and Labrador* (London, 1770?), based on maps by James Cook, Michael Lane, and Joseph Gilbert; James Cook's atlas accompanying *An Account of the Voyages ... for Making Discoveries in the Southern Hemisphere ...* (London, 1773); Jean François de Galaup, Comte de Lapérouse's *Atlas du voyage de La Pérouse* (Paris, 1797), which contains maps of "all the lands which had escaped the vigilance of Cook"; George Vancouver's atlas accompanying *Voyage of Discovery to the North Pacific Ocean and Round the World* (London, 1798); Mikhail Teben'kov's *Atlas sieverozapadnykh beregov Ameriki ot Beringova proliva do mysa Korríentes i ostrovov Aleutskikh* [Atlas of the Northwest Coasts of America from the Bering Strait to Cape Corrientes and the Aleutian Islands] (St. Petersburg, 1852), prepared by the former governor of Russian Alaska, which provided the best charts of the Pacific coast of the United States until 1854; Charles Wilkes's atlas of charts accompanying his report on the U.S. Exploring Expedition (Philadelphia, 1858), the first scientific maritime exploring expedition sponsored by the federal government.

Plans of cities, towns, and private estates have been bound in atlas format since the sixteenth century. The division is fortunate to have an excellent copy of the earliest atlas devoted to city plans, Antoine du Pinet's *Plantz, povrtraitz, et descriptions de plvsievrs villes et forteresses, tant de l'Evrope, Asie, & Afrique, que des Indes, & terrees neuues*, published in Lyon in 1564. It also has copies of both the Latin and French editions of Georg Braun and Franz Hogenberg's *Civitates orbis terrarvm*, the first systematic city atlas, which was published in six parts from 1572 to 1618. Containing 350 plans and views of most of the leading cities of the world, the French edition is generally considered the most magnificent city atlas. One of the most beautifully engraved and hand-colored atlases in the division is Joan Blaeu's *Theatrvm civitatvm et admirandorvm Italiæ* (Amsterdam, 1663), a two-volume collection of architectural drawings, statues, and landscape views in Italy, Piedmont, and Savoy. Considered among the finest topographical works ever published, only a small number were printed. Several manuscript estate atlases are also found in the collections that document the real estate holdings of the landed gentry in England.

With the advent of lithography and other modern printing techniques, the number of atlases published during the nineteenth and twentieth centuries increased dramatically. Consequently, the Library's holdings of atlases from the last two centuries is voluminous (constituting over 90 percent of the atlas collection). These holdings include general world atlases, regional volumes for all countries and many states, counties, and cities, military atlases, and special purpose or thematic atlases devoted to a wide variety of cultural, economic, historical, and scientific subjects.

The prenineteenth-century practice of publishing world and regional atlases that included general reference maps of the world, continents, and individual countries proliferated during the nineteenth and twentieth centuries as publishers attempted to reach large, general audiences. The division's holdings are particularly strong in terms of general world atlases issued by American, British, and German nineteenth-century publishers. The United States, which did not enter the atlas publishing business until the end of the eighteenth century, is represented by Mathew Carey, Jedidiah Morse, John Melish, Henry S. Tanner, Fielding Lucas, Anthony Finley, S. Augustus Mitchell, G. Woolworth Colton, Alvin J. Johnson, George F. Cram, and Rand McNally and Company. Some of the more prominent British publishers include Aaron Arrowsmith, John Bartholomew, Alexander K. Johnston, and George Philip. German holdings include the works of Richard Andree, Ernst Debes, Heinrich Kiepert, Justus Perthes, and Adolf Stieler. In the case of the last publisher, the Library holds over thirty-five editions or variant issues of his *Hand-Atlas über alle Theile der Erde* (Gotha, 1816–1937), including a rare photocopy of the 1937 edition reprinted by the U.S. Office of Strategic Services after 1943.

In addition to the fire insurance maps and atlases described in the Special Collections chapter, the division holds a large number of large-scale city real estate atlases. Prepared for tax assessment and sales purposes, these atlases depict the size, shape, and construction material of individual buildings; lot boundaries and identification; and sometimes property ownership.

While city atlases served a specialized clientele, their rural counterparts,

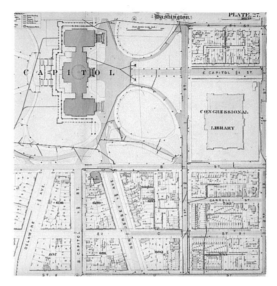

During the last two decades of the nineteenth century, Griffith Morgan Hopkins and others published detailed city atlases including this 1887 atlas of Washington, D.C. This detail from a sheet of the U.S. Capitol and vicinity includes the outline of the planned Library of Congress which was not completed until ten years later. The home of the Librarian of Congress, Ainsworth R. Spofford, is identified at the northeast corner of block 691. *(Atlas Collection)*

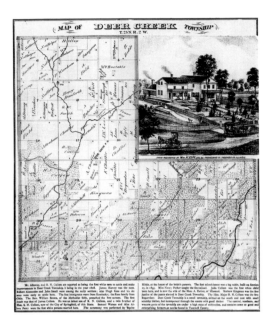

Hand-colored lithographic map of Deer Creek Township in Tazewell County, Illinois, showing names of individual landowners, along with a stylized view of a prosperous farmstead in a nearby township. Published in 1873 by the firm of Alfred T. Andreas, one of the pioneers in the development of illustrated county and state atlases, this atlas is representative of the county land ownership atlases which became popular during the last half of the nineteenth century. *(Atlas Collection)*

known as county landownership atlases, were a commercial enterprise promoted by subscription campaigns and directed to a wider audience. Based on the pre-Civil War production of wall-sized, single-sheet county landownership maps, atlases showing landownership developed into a popular atlas format starting in the 1860s in the northeastern United States, and expanding into the midwestern states by the 1870s and 1880s. These commercially published atlases contain cadastral or landownership maps for the individual townships within a county. In addition, they often include county and township histories, personal and family biographies and portraits, and views of important buildings, residences, farms, or prized livestock. The division holds more than 1,800 county landownership atlases.

The rise of thematic or special purpose cartography, which focuses on mapping the distribution of single or multiple interrelated phenomena, had its origins in the advances in the natural sciences in the late eighteenth and early nineteenth centuries, particularly with the collection of vast amounts of scientific data and the search for innovative techniques of presenting this data graphically. Examples of early physical geography atlases in the Library include Alexander von Humboldt's *Atlas géographique et physique du royaume de la Nouvelle-Espagne* (Paris, 1811), which records his observations during a 1799 to 1804 expedition to South and Central America; Heinrich Berghaus's three-volume *Physikalischer Atlas* (Gotha, 1845–1848), the first atlas to portray the physical geography of the world; Alexander Keith Johnston's *Physical Atlas* (Edinburgh, 1848), an English adaptation of the Berghaus atlas; and Traugott Broome's *Atlas zu Alex. v. Humboldt's Kosmos* [Stuttgart, 1851–1853], which was prepared to accompany Humboldt's five-volume *Kosmos*, a complete physical geography of the universe.

The focus of thematic atlases expanded to include the broad geographical topics of population, culture, agriculture, land use, and transportation. In the United States, the first atlases focusing exclusively on population were the U.S. Census Office's *Statistical Atlas of the United States Based on the Results of the Ninth Census 1870* (New York, 1874), compiled by Francis A. Walker, and *Scribner's Statistical Atlas of the United States* (New York, 1883), compiled by Fletcher W. Hewes and Henry H. Gannett from the 1880 census. Subsequent statistical atlases were published by the U.S. Census Office for the 1890, 1900, 1910, and 1920 censuses. In recent years, more specialized atlases have appeared including such topics as religion, archaeology, skiing, water management, and ocean resources.

Following the Civil War, a number of important atlases, copies of which are found in the division's holdings, were issued by various agencies of the fed-

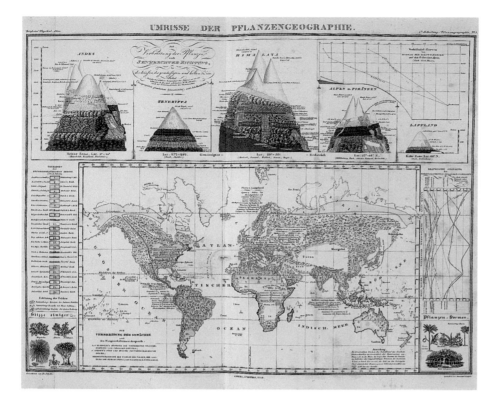

Map of botanical geography, derived from the work of German geographer Alexander von Humboldt and Danish botanist Joakim Frederik Schouw, is from Heinrich Berghaus's three-volume *Physikalischer Atlas* (Gotha, 1845), the first atlas to portray the physical geography of the world. Consisting of some ninety maps, the atlas is divided into eight sections: meteorology and climatology, hydrology and hydrography, geology, earth magnetism, botanical geography, zoological geography, anthropogeography, and ethnography. *(Atlas Collection)*

eral government. Several of these were associated with the renewed interest in exploring, surveying, and mapping the American West. In the period from 1867 to 1879, the federal government sponsored four topographical and geological surveys of the region. Commonly referred to as the Wheeler, King, Hayden, and Powell surveys, these four great western surveys produced volumes of geologic, economic, and ethnographic information as well as the first topographic and geologic atlases of the region.

Although atlases of single countries or specific regions have been published periodically since the late sixteenth century, it is only within the past eighty or ninety years that the national atlas, with an array of detailed reference and thematic maps of the country, has appeared. The publication of such atlases, most of which are represented in the division's holdings, was made possible by the extension of topographical surveys, development of new earth science disciplines, and the increase in statistical gathering techniques. One of the first to describe comprehensively a land and its people was the *Atlas de Finlande* (Helsinki, 1899). Consisting of thirty-two plates, printed in French, the atlas focused on Finland's physical environment, history, population, and communication network. Setting the standard for other national atlases produced in the twentieth century, it is

THE GRAND CAÑON AT THE FOOT OF THE TOROWEAP–LOOKING EAST

Panoramic view of the Grand Canyon by William H. Holmes from Capt. Clarence E. Dutton's *Atlas to Accompany the Monograph on the Tertiary History of the Grand Cañon District* (Washington, 1882). The leading scientific illustrator of topographic and geologic phenomena for the Great Western Surveys following the Civil War, Holmes later became the first director of the National Gallery of Art in Washington. (*Atlas Collection*)

now in its fifth edition under the title of *Suomen Kartasto/Atlas over Finland/Atlas of Finland* (Helsinki, 1977). With the fall of the Chinese monarchy and the establishment of the Republic in 1911 to 1912, Wen-chiang Ting's *Chung-hua min kuo hsin ti t'u* [New Atlas of the Republic of China] (Shanghai, 1934) documented many geographical changes that were not previously known outside that country. Although the atlas received relatively wide distribution in Western countries, its usefulness was limited until the Geography and Map Division published a translation in 1949, *A Supplementary Key to Accompany the V. K. Ting Atlas of China (Edition of 1934)*.

After World War II, there was an enormous increase in both the number and quality of national and regional atlases, and in the United States, France, and Canada, particularly of state and provincial atlases. While the pre-twentieth-century atlases were produced by individual cartographers, geographers, commercial publishing firms, or geographical societies, the more recent ones have been prepared by government agencies with large, skilled cartographic staffs. The

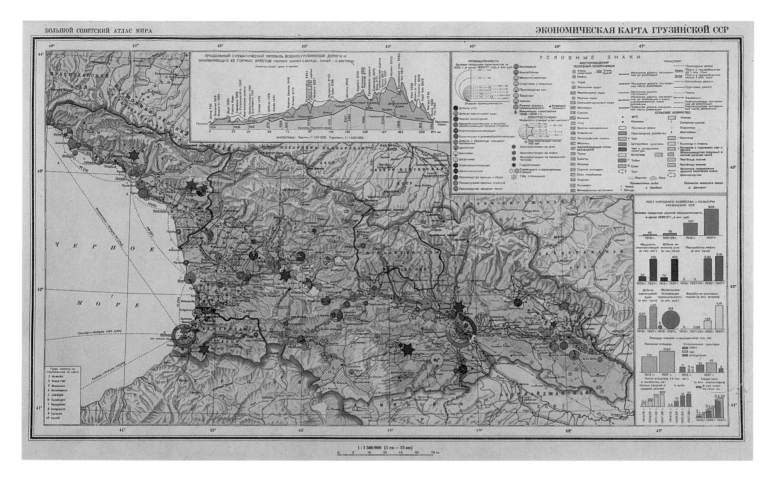

contents of these atlases have evolved from the general, richly decorated early maps to the comprehensive reference works of today that include not only topographic maps but many different kinds of thematic maps in which the latest innovative graphic design concepts are employed. The first comprehensive and uniformly designed national atlas of the Untied States was the U.S. Geological Survey's *National Atlas of the United States of America* (Washington, D.C., 1970), which was edited by Arch C. Gerlach, Chief of the Geography and Map Division from 1950 to 1967. Representative of other national atlases published during the last thirty years is *The National Atlas of Japan* (Tokyo, 1977), which was issued simultaneously in Japanese and English. Outstanding examples of modern state and provincial atlases are William G. Loy's *Atlas of Oregon* (Eugene, 1976), which was compiled with the cooperation of state universities and colleges, and state and federal agencies, and *Economic Atlas of Ontario* (Toronto, 1969), which was a cooperative enterprise of the University of Toronto and the Ontario Department of Economics and Development.

The economic map of the former Georgian Soviet Socialist Republic from the *Bol'shoi sovetskii atlas mira* [Great Soviet World Atlas] (Moscow, 1937–1939). Issued just before World War II, this atlas was withdrawn from circulation by Soviet authorities since it contained many detailed maps of the Soviet Union. The Office of Strategic Services issued a color facsimile in 1943 from one of two copies obtained by the U.S. government before the atlas was restricted. The Geography and Map Division has copies of both the original publication and the 1943 facsimile. (*Atlas collection*)

Special Collections

THE GEOGRAPHY AND MAP DIVISION maintains more than one hundred individual collections that have been acquired through gifts, government transfers, and purchases or assembled by division specialists according to common themes. In addition, the Vault Map Collection includes some three thousand manuscript and rare printed maps that have been filed together for their intrinsic, artistic, or historical significance. With few exceptions, these collections are stored in a specially designed vault equipped with temperature and humidity controls.

A number of individual rare maps and collections are noteworthy for their association with presidents of the United States, several of whom began their careers as surveyors or displayed some skill as cartographers, such as George Washington, Thomas Jefferson, and Millard Fillmore. The collections of two twentieth-century presidents, Theodore Roosevelt and Woodrow Wilson, reflect the expanding role of the presidency on the international scene. Other presidents associated with maps in the special collections include John Quincy Adams, James Buchanan, Abraham Lincoln, William McKinley, James Monroe, and Franklin Roosevelt.

One of the great treasures of the division is associated with the first and third presidents. Pierre Charles L'Enfant's original plan for the capital of the United States was compiled under the direction of Washington and extensively annotated by Jefferson. Submitted to President Washington on August 26, 1791, this event was commemorated by the Library two centuries later, on August 26, 1992, with the publication of a full-color facsimile reproduction and a newly created computer-generated (digitized) version of the plan. Entitled *Plan of the City Intended for the Permanent Seat of the Government of the Untied States,* L'Enfant's plan forms the cornerstone of the Library's unrivalled collection of maps and atlases of the city of Washington, D.C. A study of the plan by Richard W. Stephenson is available under the title *"A Plan Whol[l]y New": Pierre Charles L'Enfant's Plan of the City of Washington* (Washington, 1993).

The geographic coverage of the division's special collections is worldwide but its primary focus is North and South America, with the strongest holdings in the general subjects of discovery and exploration, settlement, and military campaigns. General descriptions of the Library's holdings relating to the European discovery and exploration of America are found in two recent publications prepared in conjunction with the Library of Congress's Quincentenary Program: Louis De Vorsey, Jr., *Keys to the Encounter: A Library of Congress Resource Guide for the Study of the Age of Discovery* (Washington, 1992) and John R. Hébert (editor), *1492: An Ongoing Voyage* (Washington, 1992). Both are well illustrated.

The division holds a small but representative collection of thirty-three portolan

With this I hand to each of you a copy of a map, compiled from the best sources, and which in the main is correct.... You all now have the same map, so that no mistakes or confusion need result from different names of localities.

MAJ.-GEN. WILLIAM TECUMSEH SHERMAN TO DIVISION COMMANDERS, DECEMBER 23, 1862.

OPPOSITE: This large manuscript map of the Kingdom of Ethiopia once hung in the palace of His Royal Highness Ras Tafari, later known as Emperor Haile Selassie I. Presented to the Library in 1924 by Homer L. Shantz, who received it personally from Ras Tafari along with "some spears, shields, and coins" while on an official U.S. mission to map African vegetation, it was prepared by the court geographer in Addis Ababa "by order of the Regent" in 1923. His Imperial Majesty was reunited with the map when he viewed it during a visit to the Library of Congress on May 28, 1954, and recalled its presentation to Dr. Shantz thirty years earlier. *(Vault Map Collection)*

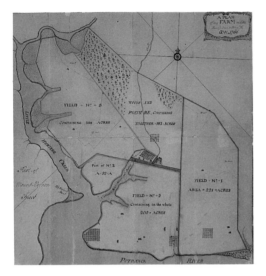

charts dating from the midfourteenth century to 1770. Portolan charts appear to have evolved from sailing guides, known as *portolanos*, during the late thirteenth century in northern Italy or in the western Mediterranean in the vicinity of Majorca or Barcelona. Hand-drawn on animal skins of parchment or vellum without borders and generally lacking titles and legends, they are characterized by a profusion of place names lettered perpendicular to the coastlines and an intersecting system of radiating lines and compass roses. Many are brightly illuminated and elaborately embellished. Among the most distinctive are an anonymous Catalan chart of the Mediterranean Sea dated before 1350 (the earliest portolan chart in the Western Hemisphere); and Samuel de Champlain's chart of his three-year exploration of the northeast coast of North America, which he drew on vellum during the winter of 1606 to 1607. The division's collection is described in *Nautical Charts on Vellum in the Library of Congress* (Washington, 1977), compiled by Walter W. Ristow and Raleigh A. Skelton.

The Library's holdings of sixteenth-century maps published during the Age of Discovery were enriched by one of its great benefactors in 1949 when Lessing J. Rosenwald donated six rare Renaissance maps including Diego Gutiérrez's celebrated map of the Western Hemisphere entitled *Americae sive qvartae orbis partis nova et exactissima descriptio* (1562) The other gifts include André Thevet's equally rare *Le Novveav monde descovvert et illvstre de nostre temps*, published in Paris in 1581; Franz Hogenberg's *Americae et proximarvm regionvm orae descriptio* (1589); Paolo Forlani's world map, *Vniversale descrittione di tvtta la terra conoscivta fin qvi*, engraved by Ferrando Bertelli (1565); and Gabriel Tatton's *Maris Pacifici*, engraved by Benjamin Wright (1600). These maps are described by Clara E. LeGear in Walter W. Ristow's (compiler) *A la Carte: Selected Papers on Maps and Atlases* (Washington, 1972). Other significant collections that pertain to the discovery and exploration of America include materials collected by Henry Harrisse, Johann Georg Kohl, and Woodbury Lowery.

The bequest of Henry Harrisse, who was both a collector and a student of the exploration of America, included fourteen manuscript maps drawn by Johannes Vingboons, cartographer to the Prince of Nassau, for the West India Company of Holland. One of these, which was entitled *Manatvs* and was "Drawn on the Spot" in 1639, is the earliest cartographic depiction of Manhattan Island. Two other noteworthy maps that were bequeathed by Harrisse are Samuel de Champlain's chart of the northeast coast of North America (mentioned above) and a map on vellum entitled *Description du pais des Hurons* by Saint Jean de Brébeuf (who was martyred by Iroquois Indians on March 16, 1649), illustrating the location of Indian tribes and Jesuit missions in the vicinity of Lake

George Washington, who was trained as a surveyor when he was a teenager, prepared this manuscript plat in 1766 of lands that he had purchased adjacent to his ancestral plantation of Mount Vernon. Known as River Farm, this was one of five farms which comprised the 8,000 acres that he owned in the vicinity of Little Hunting Creek, less than ten miles south of Alexandria, Virginia. *(Vault Map Collection)*

Huron. Information about this collection is provided by Richard W. Stephenson, "The Henry Harrisse Collection of Publications, Papers, and Maps Pertaining to the Early Exploration of America," published in *Terrae Incognitae* (volume 16, Detroit, 1984).

Complementing Harrisse is the Johann Georg Kohl Collection of 474 annotated manuscript facsimile maps relating to the discovery and exploration of the New World from 1500 to 1834. These maps were copied by the nineteenth-century German geographer Johann Georg Kohl from "old books" and collections in Germany, France, and England. The maps are listed by Justin Winsor in *The Kohl Collection (now in the Library of Congress) of Maps Relating to America, with an Index by Philip Lee Phillips* (Washington, 1904). Additional information about Kohl is found in John A. Wolter, "Johann Georg Kohl and America," *The Map Collector* (volume 17, Tring, England, December 1981), and Hans-Albrecht Koch, Margrit B. Krewson, and John A. Wolter (ed.), *Progress of Discovery: Johann Georg Kohl* (Graz, Austria, 1993).

The Lowery Collection of maps was bequeathed to the Congressional Library by Woodbury Lowery on July 5, 1905 "hoping they might there be most accessible to students." A prominent Washington patent lawyer, Lowery travelled throughout Europe collecting books and maps for his avocation, a scholarly study of the cartography of early Spanish settlement in the Western Hemisphere, which was edited by Philip Lee Phillips and published under the title *The Lowery Collection: A Descriptive List of Maps of the Spanish Possessions within the Present Limits of the United States, 1502–1820* (Washington, 1912).

For the student of nineteenth-century exploration of the American West, the division has particularly rich holdings. The Lewis and Clark Collection is indispensable for understanding the early mapping of this region. Transferred in 1925 from the files of the Office of Indian Affairs, Department of the Interior, the collection consists of twelve manuscript maps associated with the planning of the Lewis and Clark overland expedition to the mouth of the Columbia River from 1803 to 1806 and activities relating to William Clark's official duties as superintendent of Indian Affairs at St. Louis from 1807 to 1813 and as governor of the Missouri Territory. A related but no less valuable item from the Vault Map Collection is Robert Frazer's large manuscript *Map of the discoveries of Capt Lewis & Clark from the Rockey mountain and the River Lewis to the Cap of Disappointement or the Coloumbia River At the North Pacific Ocean*. A member of the Corps of Discovery, Frazer prepared this map in 1806 to accompany his own journal of the expedition, which was never published. Later, the map came into the possession of John Henry

Detail from computer-generated version of Pierre Charles L'Enfant's original plan for the capital of the United States, enhanced to show Thomas Jefferson's handwritten editorial changes. Compiled in 1791 under the direction of Pres. George Washington, this plan still guides the planning of the central core of Washington, D.C. An architect and military engineer, the French born L'Enfant joined the Continental Army and spent the winter of 1777 to 1778 at Valley Forge, where he first met Washington. L'Enfant's plan was transferred to the Library of Congress by the U.S. Army Corps of Engineers in 1918 and has recently been restored by the Library's Conservation Office and sealed in a case filled with argon gas. (*Vault Map Collection*)

One of the great cartographic treasures of the Library, this explorer's chart of the northeast coast of North America from Cape Sable to Cape Cod was drawn by Samuel de Champlain in 1607. *(Henry Harrisse Collection)*

Alexander, the first Maryland state cartographer, and was obtained in 1922 by the Library from the estate of Alexander's son.

Much of the trans-Mississippi west was explored and mapped by military officers of the U.S. Army's Corps of Topographical Engineers and, after the Civil War, by civilian scientists of the Interior Department whose final reports and maps were published by Congress. Normally bound in House and Senate documents, the maps are often difficult to use because of their large format and fragile nature. Many of these maps, which are in the division's Congressional Serial

Diego Gutiérrez's celebrated map of the Western Hemisphere entitled *Americae sive qvartae orbis partis nova et exactissima descriptio.* One of two known copies, it was engraved by the great Flemish artist Hieronymus Cock in 1562 and has the distinction of being the first map to carry the name California. At one time it was owned by the Duke of Gotha. *(Vault Map Collection)*

Set Collection, are described and reproduced in Carl Wheat's monumental five-volume work, *Mapping the Transmississippi West* (San Francisco, 1957–1963). Related material is found in the Gilbert Thompson Collection.

Three significant historical maps of vital importance to the history of the United States were made the special focus of Lawrence Martin's desiderata list during his tenure as Chief of the Geography and Map Division from 1924 to 1946. An authority on boundary problems and a consultant to the State Department, Martin collected these maps for their value in illuminating issues relating to

One of three original maps depicting the maritime explorations of the coasts of the United States, this historical chart of the Atlantic Coast was compiled by the German geographer Johann Georg Kohl in 1856 for the U.S. Coast Survey. The different colored lines indicate the extent of the coast visited by the various explorers. (*Johann Georg Kohl Collection*)

boundary disputes. Each has been brought together as a separate collection under the names of the authors of these maps: John Mitchell, John Melish, and John Disturnell. Lists of all three maps are found in *A la Carte*.

Division holdings are particularly rich sources for the study of the French and Indian War and the American Revolution. Numbering more than two thousand titles, including six hundred original manuscript drawings, they represent the work of the leading British, French, and American eighteenth-century cartographers and publishers. A list of maps covering this period was compiled by John R. Sellers and Patricia Molen Van Ee as part of the Library's American Revolution Bicentennial program under the title *Maps and Charts of North America and the West Indies, 1750–1789: A Guide to the Collections in the Library of Congress* (Washington, 1981). Particularly valuable for the study of military mapping during the war are the following collections: Peter Force, William Faden, Rochambeau, Richard Howe, and Pierre Ozanne. Supplementing this material are photostatic copies of the maps prepared by the surveyors-general of the Continental Army, Robert Erskine and Simeon DeWitt, obtained from the New-York Historical Society, and the Duke of Cumberland Map Collection on microfiche from the Royal Library in Windsor Castle.

A unique form of cartographic artifact during the colonial era was the powder horn map. Embellishing powder horns with maps was a popular activity with soldiers serving in British Colonial America, especially during the French and Indian War and the American Revolutionary War. The division's collection includes five horns of British origin dating from the French and Indian War era, three American ones engraved during the Revolutionary War, and one believed to have been made or carried by a Pennsylvania frontiersman some time between 1790 and 1810. Several of the horns include the names of their owners.

Manuscript maps relating to Andrew Jackson's military campaigns during the War of 1812 and postwar activities with the Creek Indians are found in the Blair Collection. These maps were originally presented to the Library in 1903 by the descendants of Francis P. Blair, Jackson's adopted son, along with his papers which are housed in the Manuscript Division. From a donation by Dr. Warren Coleman of New York City in 1936, the division acquired a manuscript map of the Battle of Horseshoe Bend which took place March 27, 1814, on the Tallapoosa River in eastern Alabama where Gen. Andrew Jackson defeated a large force of Creek Indians. This map was compiled by Dr. Coleman's ancestor, a regimental quartermaster, who drew it "upon his hat the morning after the battle."

The American Civil War remains one of the most active topics of research

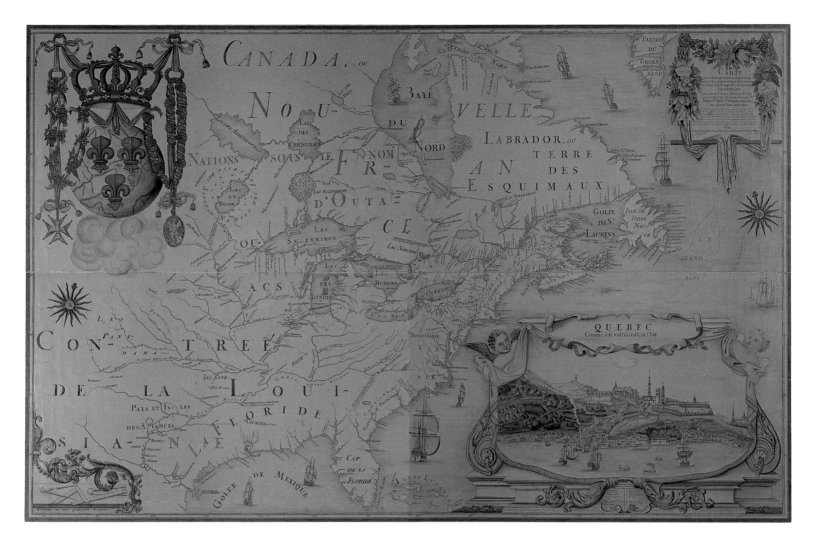

in the Geography and Map Division. Fortunately for the researcher, the Library of Congress has the finest collection of Civil War printed maps and the foremost collection of Confederate field maps, numbering more than 2,300 maps and atlases. An additional 162 maps from twenty-eight collections are found in the Library's Manuscript Division. These materials are described in Richard W. Stephenson's *Civil War Maps: An Annotated List of Maps and Atlases in the Library of Congress* (Washington, 1989). Included are topographic sketch maps showing the approximate terrain or routes of potential conflict, maps depicting the theater of military operations, order-of-battle maps showing the location of command units, strategic maps used in the planning and execution of campaigns, and commercial and newspaper maps designed to persuade and inform the public. The American Civil War also witnessed the introduction of reproduction techniques

Jean-Baptiste Louis Franquelin's *Carte de l'Amérique Septentrionale* was originally compiled in Quebec in 1688. As the official court cartographer for the governor of New France from 1678 to 1700, Franquelin had access to the reports prepared by returning frontier missionaries and explorers. This copy was made for the Library of Congress between 1909 and 1910 from the original in *Archives du Dépôt des Cartes de la Marine*. Franquelin's maps were never published. *(Vault Map Collection)*

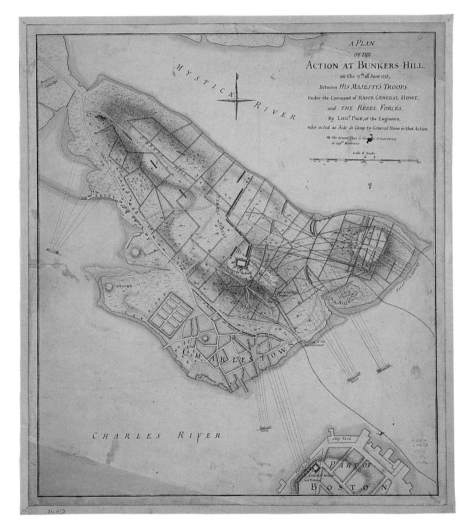

TOP: During the French and Indian War and the American Revolution, soldiers often embellished their powder horns with maps and other images. The more elaborate works are thought to have been prepared as campaign souvenirs for British officers. The St. Lawrence River and the cities of Quebec and Montreal are depicted on this powder horn. *(Powder Horn Collection)*

BOTTOM: The Battle of Bunker Hill, the first major battle of the American Revolution, is depicted in this manuscript plan by an aide to the leader of the British troops, Gen. William Howe. The map was later acquired by William Faden, geographer to King George III and foremost British map publisher of the late eighteenth century. *(William Faden Collection)*

OPPOSITE: Sketch map of the battlefield of Gettysburg by Jedediah Hotchkiss, chief topographer of the Confederate Army of Northern Virginia, shows troop positions, July 1–2, 1863. Confederate divisions and corps are named, but Federal commands are not named. *(Jedediah Hotchkiss Collection)*

such as sunprints, photography, and lithography to keep up with the great demand for maps.

The finest collections of Confederate maps available today is the Jedediah Hotchkiss Collection. Acquired in 1948 from Mrs. R. E. Christian, granddaughter of Maj. Jedediah Hotchkiss, chief topographer of the Army of Northern Virginia, it consists of manuscript field sketches, reconnaissance maps, county maps, regional maps, and battle maps. The centerpiece of the collection is a large, table-size detailed drawing of the Shenandoah Valley surveyed and compiled at the request of Gen. Thomas J. "Stonewall" Jackson for his spring campaign of 1862. A computer-enhanced (digitized) version of this map has been recently reproduced by the U.S. Park Service as an aid to its management of historic sites in the Shenandoah Valley. The Confederate collection has been enhanced by photostatic copies of seventy-five unique manuscript maps from the Military Academy at West Point, the Virginia Historical Society, and the College of William and Mary. These map were prepared for Gen. Jeremy F. Gilmer, chief of the Confederate engineers. Other collections that pertain to the Civil War include William Tecumseh Sherman, Orlando M. Poe, Nathaniel Prentiss Banks, Samuel P. Heintzelman, and George B. McClellan. Also of interest are maps that belonged to Gen. Joshua Lawrence Chamberlain, whose heroism at Gettysburg has been featured by Michael Shaara in *The Killer Angels* (New York, 1974), a Pulitzer-Prize winning account of the four-day battle which was made into the movie *Gettysburg* (1993). The map collection was donated by Eleanor Wyllys Allen, Chamberlain's granddaughter. It includes maps related to Gettysburg, Petersburg, and Five Forks. A group of thirty one maps illustrate the operations of the Armies of the Potomac and James from May 4, 1864, to April 9, 1865.

Cartographic materials that document the development and growth of urban America are extensive and unequaled. Through copyright deposits, government transfers, and exchanges, the division has acquired the nation's foremost collection of city maps issued by fire insurance companies and underwriters. Developed in London in the 1790s and first published in the United States by the Jefferson Insurance Company of New York City in the 1850s, fire insurance maps are large-scale maps designed to provide insurance underwriters with detailed information concerning fire risks for individual residential and commercial properties. They depict street patterns, water systems, lot lines, individual buildings and construction material. Their historical value is enhanced by updated editions.

By far, the largest number of fire insurance maps is found in the Sanborn Map Company Collection which contains 600,000 sheets representing 12,000 American

OPPOSITE TOP: A manuscript map of the region from Lake Erie to the mouth of the Ohio River drawn about 1755 by "Chegeree (the Indian) who says he has travelled through the country." *(Vault Map Collection)*

OPPOSITE BOTTOM: The first map to show the region that is now part of Yellowstone National Park. Drawn by Pierre-Jean DeSmet for Col. Donald D. Mitchell, Superintendent of Indian Affairs for the St. Louis Department, it was used during the 1851 Fort Laramie Treaty negotiations to show boundaries for the northern plains Indian tribes. A Belgian Jesuit missionary who had traveled through much of the Oregon country and the Great Plains establishing Catholic missions, Father DeSmet compiled a number of important maps of the region. The information for this map was furnished to DeSmet by Jim Bridger, the famous guide and fur trapper who led or directed at least seven trapping and hunting parties through the region between 1835 and 1850. *(Vault Map Collection)*

FALLS ON ARIZONA CANAL

OFFICE OF THE
DAILY PHOENIX HERALD
R. A. MORFORD
EDITOR AND
PROPR.

BIRD'S EYE VIEW of
PHOENIX
MARICOPA CO.
ARIZONA.

VIEW LOOKING NORTH-EAST.

Sketched by
C. J. DYER,
PHŒNIX, A.T.

REFERENCES.

1 County Court House.
2 Baptist Church.
3 Washington St. Methodist Church.
4 Public School House.
5 Centre St. Methodist Church.
6 Salt River Valley Canal.
7 Residence of J. T. Simms.
8 Gazette Printing Office.
9 Kales & Lewis' Bank.
10 Valley Bank.
11 Herald Printing Office.
12 J. Y. T. Smith's Flour Mill.
13 Public Plaza.
14 Irvine Building.
15 Phoenix Swimming Baths.
16 Phoenix Hotel, Chas. Salari, Prop.
17 Gregory House & Lumber Yard.
18 Hotel Lemon.
19 Catholic Church.
20 Dutch Ditch.
21 Maricopa Canal.
22 Grand Canal.
23 Arizona Canal.
24 Residence of H. H. McNeil.
25 Residence of M. W. Kales.
26 Property of E. B. Kirkland.
27 Lount Bros.' Ice Factory.
28 F. Miner's Lumber Yard.
29 H. W. Ryder's Lumber Yard.

COPYRIGHTED BY C. J. DYER, PHŒNIX, ARIZONA, 1885.

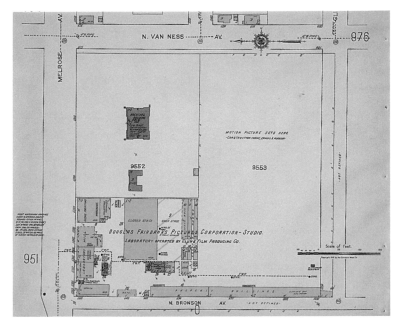

ABOVE: The Sanborn Map Company prepared detailed maps of some 12,000 American cities for fire insurance underwriters, including this detail from a sheet showing the Douglas Fairbanks Pictures Corporation Studio in Los Angeles as it appeared in 1919. These maps are color-coded to depict building materials. (*Sanborn Map Collection*)

LEFT: Panoramic view of Phoenix, Arizona by C. J. Dyer in 1885. Compiled from drawings by topographic artists who walked the streets, these detailed bird's-eye perspectives are one expression of the optimism of urban life during the Victorian era. (*MARC Map Collection*)

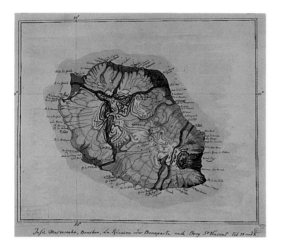

Infel Mascarenha, Bourbon, La Réunion oder Bonaparte nach Berry St Vincent Tab 14 und 15

ABOVE: This map of Réunion Island in the Indian Ocean is one of forty manuscript maps and views of volcanoes drawn by the nineteenth-century German geographer Carl Ritter and collected by Franz Ritter von Hauslab, an Austro-Hungarian military officer, cartographer, and ardent map collector. *(Hauslab-Liechtenstein Map Collection)*

OPPOSITE: Land litigation map of Oztoticpac, a royal Aztec estate in the city of Texcoco near present-day Mexico City. Hand-drawn by one or more Aztec Indians in 1540, it was prepared to show the lands and properties of Don Carlos Chichimecatecotl, a converted Texcocan noble executed in 1539 by Spanish officials during the Inquisition for retaining Aztec spiritual relics. Although primarily a pictorial document, it is annotated in Spanish and Nahuatl, the Aztec language. *(Vault Map Collection)*

cities dated from 1876 to the 1970s. The bulk of these maps were deposited by the company as copyright deposits, but about one-third were transferred from the Commerce Department's Bureau of the Census in 1967, which originally purchased the maps at a cost of one-half million dollars. The Census Bureau maps contain paste-on correction sheets to reflect changes such as the construction or demolition of individual buildings. The entire collection is available on 35mm black and white microfilm from Chadwyk-Healy, Inc. and is described in *Fire Insurance Maps in the Library of Congress: Plans of North American Cities and Towns Produced by the Sanborn Map Company* (Washington, 1981). Other fire insurance holdings include the work of H. Bennett, the Charles E. Goad Company, Ernest Hexamer, the Minnesota and Dakota Fire Underwriters Company, Charles Rascher, and Alphonso Whipple. All of these companies were eventually absorbed by Sanborn, Inc.

The Geography and Map Division has extensive holdings of panoramic maps of North American cities and towns. Also known as bird's-eye views, perspective maps, or panoramic views, these maps provide unique images of cities as viewed at an oblique angle from an elevation of 2,000 to 3,000 feet. Prepared by artist-cartographers who walked the streets sketching buildings and major landscape features, they were used to promote a city's commercial and residential potential. Although the division has more than 1,800 panoramic views, they continue to be acquired. Dating from 1837 to the 1920s, panoramic views depict a wide variety of urban features such as streets, hotels, houses, mills and factories, court houses, schools and colleges, railway depots and round-houses, fair grounds, cemeteries, canals, bridges, gas works, ferries, race courses, lumber yards, hospitals, banks, and churches. Many include insets of architectural renderings of private homes, commercial and public establishments, and industrial plants. Two special collections particularly rich for the study of small town America during the Victorian Age are those of Albert Ruger, a Prussian immigrant who began drawing views while serving with the Ohio Volunteers during the Civil War, and Thaddeus Mortimer Fowler whose career spanned almost the entire era, from 1870 to 1922. The division has 224 of the 301 separate views attributed to Fowler, covering eighteen states and Canada. More than one hundred views were presented to the division from 1970 to 1971 by the artist's daughter-in-law, Mrs. T. B. Fowler, and her family. Other cartographic-artists and panoramic publishers represented in the collections are Oakley H. Bailey, Lucien R. Burleigh, Augustus Koch, and Henry Wellge. A checklist of the Geography and Map Division's holdings is found in *Panoramic Maps of Cities in the United States and Canada*, compiled by John R. Hébert and revised by Patrick E. Dempsey (Washington, 1984).

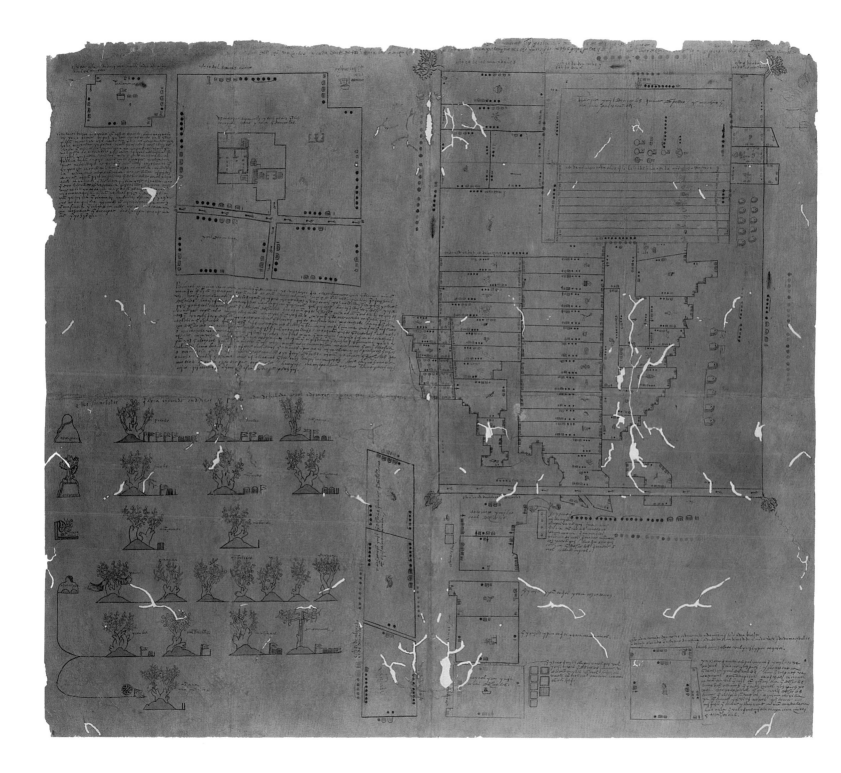

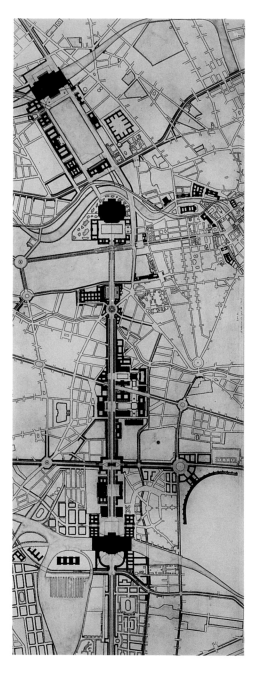

While the Geography and Map Division's special collections focus primarily on North America, coverage is worldwide. Particularly noteworthy is a small but representative collection of large seventeenth-century decorative wall maps of the world that were produced by leading Dutch, French, and Italian publishing houses to meet the growing demand for attractive wall hangings by an emerging middle class. Due to their size, few wall maps have survived the ravages of time. Of the 125 recorded copies, the division has eighteen. Beginning in 1608, the Dutch cartographer Willem Janszoon Blaeu first published a set of separate wall maps of the four continents. Through the generosity of Hans P. Kraus, the division has copies of African, Asian, and European maps reprinted by the Visscher firm about 1657. The Kraus gift also included a rare set of four continental maps and a map of the world published by the Joachim Ottens publishing house in Amsterdam dedicated to William and Mary, who reigned from 1689 to 1702. Only one other set of these five maps preserved together is known. In addition, the wall map collection includes a set of Blaeu's 1608 four continental maps reissued in Bologna in 1673 by Pietro Todeschi, a noted engraver of perspective views; an unrecorded French edition of Blaeu's wall map of Africa, published by Hubert Jaillot in 1669; and a reengraving in Italy by Guiseppe Longhi and Carlo Scotti about 1680 of the first edition of Frederik de Wit's giant wall map of the world, originally published in Amsterdam in 1660.

Maps and charts of Latin and South America are well represented. The oldest and most remarkable is a land litigation map of Oztoticpac, a royal Aztec estate in the city of Texcoco near present-day Mexico City. This map has been analyzed by Howard F. Cline in *A la Carte*. Other milestones of Spanish colonial cartography in Latin America include Juan de la Cruz Cano's rare *Mapa geográfico de America meridional* (Madrid, 1775), an eight-sheet wall map whose sale was suppressed by Spanish authorities shortly after publication; William Faden's facsimile of the 1775 Cruz Cano map published in 1799 in London at the request of Thomas Jefferson; and Nicolas de Lafora's manuscript copy of *Mapa de toda la frontera de los dominios del rey en la America septentrional*, originally compiled in 1771 to show Mexico's northern frontier. Another manuscript version of Lafora's map is part of the Gen. Peter H. Hagner Collection.

Special collections that relate primarily to Latin and South America were assembled by John Barrett, director of the Pan American Union, 1894 to 1920; the Panama Canal Zone Library-Museum; the Portuguese-Spanish Boundary Commission, described in Lawrence Martin and Walter W. Ristow's "South American Historical Maps" in *A la Carte*; the Maggs Collection of early Spanish nautical charts; and Ephraim George Squier, an American journalist engaged in diplomatic and archeologic work in Central America and Peru from 1849 to 1865. The maps prepared by Squier are described by John R. Hébert in the *Quarterly Journal of the Library of Congress* (volume 29, Washington, January 1972).

One of the prized additions to the division is the Hauslab-Liechtenstein Map Collection which includes some eight thousand manuscript and printed maps primarily related to Europe with special emphasis on the Austro-Hungarian Empire and its separate provinces. Assembled by Franz Ritter von Hauslab, a member of the Austrian nobility and a distinguished military engineer who fought with Russian forces against Napoleon Bonaparte's armies, the collection reflects his life-long interests in military affairs, the application of lithography to map printing, the portrayal of terrain on maps, and thematic mapping. The major categories include maps of European cities; military fortification plans; battle maps depicting most of the major European conflicts of the seventeenth through the nineteenth centuries; medium- and large-scale topographic map series; maps and views of volcanoes; panoramic and perspective maps; geologic and geognostic maps; language and ethnographic maps; and facsimiles and tracings which illustrate the history of cartography. The nineteenth century was a time for testing new printing technologies, all of which are represented. These include examples of wood-block printing, copperplate engraving, lithography, chromolithography, photolithography, zincography, heliogravure, sun prints, and transfers. In addition, the collection includes a number of manuscript maps and views of Italy prepared by Carl Ritter, a leading nineteenth-century German geographer, whose library was purchased by Hauslab in 1861.

While the majority of the division's maps relating to World War I and World War II are found among the division's general collections, several special collections contain pertinent material, such as that of World War I Gen. Charles Pelot Summerall, commander of the 4th, 5th, and 9th Army Corps in France; the Nazi geographer Karl Haushofer; and Albert Speer, Hitler's armaments minister and personal architect.

Although the coastal outline of Africa was one of the first continents charted by European cartographers, the mapping of that continent's interior did not begin in earnest until after World War II. The only collection related specifically to Africa comprises maps acquired with the records of the American Colonization Society, an organization that assisted Black Americans in settling in Liberia during the nineteenth century. For further information on this collection and other cartographic material relating to African Americans, see Debra Newman

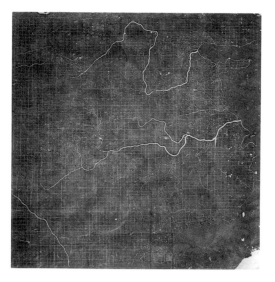

ABOVE: A rubbing taken from a 4,000-year-old stone tablet in Sian, the ancient capital of China, represents one of the oldest extant maps. Made in 1935 by Prof. W. B. Pettus of the College of Chinese Studies at Peking and given to the Library by George B. Cressey, Professor of Geography, Syracuse University, the map was apparently prepared for pedagogical purposes. It delineates the provinces of China which paid tribute to Emperor Yu, the founder in 2205 B.C. of the first legendary dynasty. *(Vault Map Collection)*

OPPOSITE: One of twenty-five hand-colored photographic plans for the rebuilding of Berlin prepared by Albert Speer, Adolph Hitler's architect, during the 1930s. *(Albert Speer Collection)*

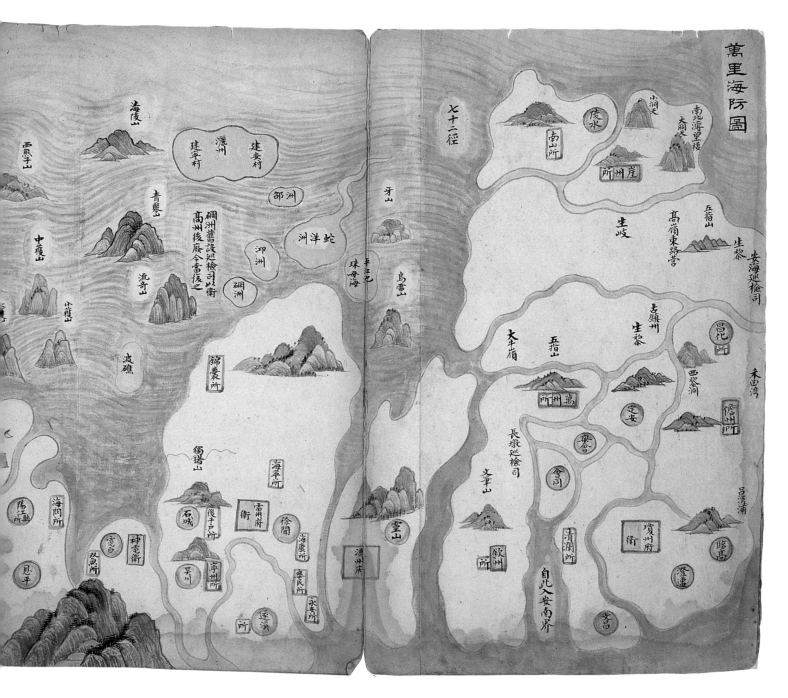

萬里海防圖

Detail of manuscript Chinese map, "Ten-Thousand-Mile Map of Maritime Defenses," drawn during the Qing Dynasty, ca. 1705. This map, which is one of eleven maps mounted in an accordion-folded album fifty-one feet in length, shows military defenses along the Chinese coast from Hainan Island to the Shandong Peninsula. (*Arthur W. Hummel Collection*)

ABOVE: Detail of Japanese manuscript scroll map (35 by 939 cm.) showing the Tokaido, the main land-sea route from Edo (Tokyo) to Nagasaki, with Fujiyama in the background. Kyoho period (1716-1736). *(Vault Map Collection)*

RIGHT: Manuscript map of Japan as viewed from Burma during World War II. This unique perspective is one of four different views drawn by Richard Edes Harrison for the December 1943 issue of *Fortune*. *(Richard Edes Harrison Collection)*

Ham (editor), *The African-American Mosaic: A Library of Congress Resource Guide for the Study of Black History and Culture* (Washington, 1993).

The student of East Asia will find the division's collection of maps of China, Korea, and Japan one of the most extensive outside of Asia. They are valuable not only for their geographical and historical insight but also because they provide students of cartography, culture, and art with artifacts that reflect a nontraditional Western European geographic mode of visual expression. Early Chinese, Korean, and Japanese maps differ from the Western European tradition in terms of the use of symbols and color, degree of pictorialization, and media and format. In an insightful article (*Asian Art*, New York, Fall 1992) based on the division's collection, the cartographic historian Cordell D. K. Yee demonstrates that the main difference between Asian and European cartography relates to the central role that art, particularly poetry, calligraphy, and landscape painting played in the development of Chinese cartography until the end of the nineteenth century.

The largest collection of rare Chinese maps was acquired through the efforts of Arthur W. Hummel, distinguished sinologist and head of the Library's Orientalia Division from 1928 to 1954, and the generosity of Andrew W. Mellon. Among the cartographic treasures are an annotated wood-block folded atlas of China from the Ming Dynasty entitled "Looking At Distant Places as if They Were on the Palm of Your Hand"; a seventeenth-century silk scroll depicting in the form of landscape paintings four important frontier regions of the Manchu dynasty, including one illustrating a clash between Russian and Manchurian troops on the Heilungkian or Amur River; and a rare wall map of the world by the Jesuit missionary Ferdinand Verbiest, engraved on eight scrolls in Peking in 1674.

Korean cartography was directly influenced by Chinese cartographic traditions that reached the peninsula during the Koryo dynasty (918–1392). The bulk of the Library's collection of rare Korean maps and atlases were acquired by two eminent educators, the archaeologist Langdon Warner, leader of the first and second China expeditions of the Fogg Museum of Harvard University, and the geographer Shannon McCune, born in Korea of American missionary parents. These collections include both manuscript copies and woodblock impressions, which generally are rarer and more valuable than manuscript copies. The division's Korean atlases range in date from circa 1760 to 1896 and are representative of the traditional hand atlases produced since early in the Yi Dynasty (1392–1910).

A number of very early rare manuscript and printed Japanese scroll maps are available for examination including one depicting the 1614 fortifications of Osaka Castle. A world map by the Japanese Buddhist scholar-priest Hotan provides an

Palestine as portrayed by cartographer-artist Hal Shelton, illustrating his unique technique for depicting landforms. Starting with an offset blue-line lithographic image of a contour map etched on a zinc printing plate, the map image was then painted with acrylic paints using an oscillating-needle airbrush. Originally designed for use by airline passengers, Shelton's maps were widely adopted for aeronautical charts and educational purposes. (*The H. M. Gousha Company Collection*)

An example of the U.S. Army Air Force's "survival" maps (printed on cloth.) This map of Luzon Island in the Philippines was issued by the Aeronautical Chart Service in April 1944. Despite the large number of cloth maps printed by British, American, and German service units during the war, very few examples of World War II cloth maps are preserved in American libraries. (*Cloth Map Collection*)

image of the Buddhist vision of world geography in terms of its cosmology. Entitled *Nansenbushu Bankoku Shoka no Zu* [Map of the Universe], it displays India, where Buddha was born, and China as the center of the world. Printed from woodcuts in 1710, this prototype map was popular in Japan until the midnineteenth century.

Most of the division's rare maps by Japanese mapmakers, however, date from the nineteenth century. A teaching collection of eleven maps assembled by Shannon McCune for use in a series of lectures he gave on Japanese geography include wood-block maps of the world, Japan, and administrative districts, one in the form of a scroll. A large-scale manuscript map of Japan shows coast lines, major rivers, roads, and terrain for the period 1816 to 1818. Drawn by Ino Tadataka, it consists of 214 sheets, with water color wash on rice paper.

Maps of Southeast Asia are found in the Minto Collection, including manuscript maps of Java, Malaccas, and Sumatra drawn by British Army engineers about 1811, just before the British invasion and annexation of Java. This collection is described by John A. Wolter in the Washington Map Society *Portolan* of April 1986. Additional maps of Southeast Asia are found in the John Barrett Collection.

While the great majority of cartographic materials housed in the Geography and Map Division are useful primarily for the information they convey about geographic place or phenomena associated with place, certain collections are also valuable for the study of the cartographic process itself. For the study of nineteenth-century map design and printing, the collections of Hauslab-Liechtenstein, Charles Rau, and Mylon Merriam are major sources of primary materials.

One of the notable contributions of American cartography was the development of the physiographic diagram or landform map. Relevant collections are those of the noted geomorphologist and teacher William Morris Davis, whose work with the block diagram technique laid the foundation for this form of cartography; Guy-Harold Smith; Erwin Raisz; Richard Edes Harrison, who began his career in journalistic cartography as a member of the staff of *Fortune* magazine in the 1930s where he developed innovative and distinctive perspective maps and landform maps that provided a generation of World War II readers with an image of the earth; Hal Shelton, whose work is found in the H. M. Gousha Collection; and Theodore R. Miller.

An excellent primary source for the study of map design in North America is a collection of competition drawings submitted to the annual American Congress on Surveying and Mapping (ACSM) Map Design Competition. Open to all map makers in the United States and Canada, the competition is sponsored by ACSM to promote concern for map design and to recognize significant design advances in cartography. Entries are judged on the basis of achievement of stated design objectives, typography, color, and craftsmanship. After winning entries are exhibited at the annual ACSM national convention, they are transferred to the Geography and Map Division for addition to the permanent map collections of the Library of Congress.

While examples of map printing artifacts are scarce, and seldom found in collections because of their vulnerability or value, the division has acquired representative examples of copper engraving plates, lithographic stones, and woodblocks in order to document the development of map printing. These are filed in the Printing Technology Collection. The scribing technique is illustrated by the recently acquired American Automobile Association Collection, which contains sixty-four printing plates for the AAA road map of Maryland, Virginia, the District of Columbia, and Delaware.

Throughout history, maps have been drawn or printed on a variety of surfaces including paper, stone, metal, wood, skin, horn, and cloth. With the development of the printing press in the midfifteenth century, however, paper became and has remained the dominant printing medium. Because of the attractiveness and durability of cloth, however, maps have been published on this material since the eighteenth century as souvenirs, as travelers' aids, and for military purposes. The Cloth Map Collection includes numerous specimens of maps printed on cloth dating from the 1790s. The earliest is a "bandanna" map depicting the plan for Washington, D.C., dated about 1793. Another fascinating early cloth map depicts the decisive battle of Waterloo, Belgium, fought June 18, 1815; it was issued shortly after the battle to commemorate the victory of the Duke of Wellington over Napoleon Bonaparte.

The largest collection of cloth maps was acquired in 1983 from the British Ministry of Defense's Mapping and Charting Establishment through the assistance of Ian Mumford, then the British Liaison Officer assigned to the U.S. Defense Mapping Agency. It consists of some sixty escape and evasion maps and air-sea rescue charts produced during World War II under the direction of the British War Office's Secret Intelligence Service, M19 for both the European and Far East theaters. This section was established on December 23, 1939, to aid in the escape and safe return to the United Kingdom of prisoners of war and men lost as sea. A set of almost fifty U.S. Army Air Force "Bailout" or "Survival Maps," issued by the Army Map Service, primarily for the Far East, are also on file. A third example of World War II cloth maps is a set of bombing target maps of cities and ports in England issued by the German General Staff, June to October 1941.

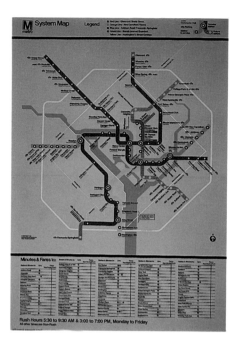

One of thirty-three translucent maps donated to the Library by the Washington Metropolitan Area Transit Authority of Washington, D.C., in 1991, it was designed to be housed in illuminated display cases in subway-station mezzanines. (*Washington Metropolitan Area Transit Authority Maps*)

PORTAGE HIGH BRIDGE.
Crossing the GENESEE River at PORTAGE, WYOMING Co. N.Y.
Built by the Buffalo and New York City R.R. Company in 1851 & '2 __ The Bridge is 800 feet long and 234 feet high.

MAP OF WYOMING COUNTY

NEWEL S. BROWN
PUBLISHER,

NEW YORK.

15 MINOR STREET
PHILADELPHIA.

FROM ACTUAL SURVEYS BY P.J.BROWN, SURVEYOR,
Author of Maps of Seneca and Monroe Counties &c.

1853.

SCALE

Entered according to Act of Congress in the Year 1853 by Robert P. Smith in the Clerks Office of the District Court of the Eastern District of Pennsylvania.

General Collections

THE DIVISION'S GENERAL COLLECTIONS, which number over 3.5 million map sheets, include both single-sheet maps and multi-sheet map series. Single-sheet maps, which provide worldwide coverage at small and medium scales, are primarily general purpose and thematic maps of continents, countries, states, counties, and cities. Multi-sheet map series, which are usually prepared at large and medium scales, also provide worldwide coverage, normally at the country and state level.

SINGLE-SHEET MAPS

More than one and a half million sheets of the division's general map holdings are composed of single-sheet maps. Over 350,000 of these, primarily those maps acquired since 1968, have been fully cataloged in the Library's computer-assisted map cataloging system (MARC). The remainder, however, which are unclassified and uncataloged, constitute a collection that is commonly known as the Titled Collection. Although there is no comprehensive listing of the individual maps in the Titled Collection, there is a basic geographic arrangement that makes it relatively easy for researchers to identify the range of maps appropriate for their examination.

The Titled Collection is representative of the history of cartography, spanning the range from finely engraved atlas plates by Ortelius to blue-line plans issued by modern city engineers. Between these two ends of the spectrum lie a fascinating array of cartographic materials. Whether received by copyright deposit, purchase, or gift, the holdings include such items as country, state, city, or county maps; panoramic views and pictorial maps; transportation maps emphasizing roads and railroads; harbor and coastal charts; military maps representing the major battles and wars; newspaper and other journalistic maps; and a broad range of thematic maps. Coverage is worldwide.

Only select portions of the Titled Collection have been described in any form, most notably in area-oriented or genre bibliographies and checklists compiled by division staff. While the richness of the collection is well appreciated, the lack of documentation leaves room for serendipitous discovery that excites readers and staff members alike. What makes the Titled Collection so valuable, however, is not just the "treasures" that are to be uncovered there. For many researchers, working with the Titled Collection can save trips to dozens of institutions. After the invention of the photostating process, the acquisition of photocopies from archives and libraries around the world became a major goal of the division. Consequently,

---

Maps break down our inhibitions, stimulate our glands, stir our imagination, loose our tongues. The map speaks across the barrier of language; it is sometimes claimed as the language of geography.

CARL O. SAUER
"The Education of a Geographer," 1956

Let us look at the map, for maps, like faces, are the signature of history.

WILL DURANT

OPPOSITE: This detail of the 1853 map of Wyoming County in the western part of New York State is typical of the large, wall-sized county maps that gained wide circulation in the northeastern United States before the Civil War. Published in Philadelphia by Newel S. Brown, this map provides coverage of the entire county showing township boundaries, roads, towns and villages, and names of land owners, as well as enlarged insets of the individual towns and villages and views of the more prominent landmarks and structures in the county. The richly decorated borders emphasize the rural and agricultural character of the county as well as the Native American origins of the county name. *(Titled Collection)*

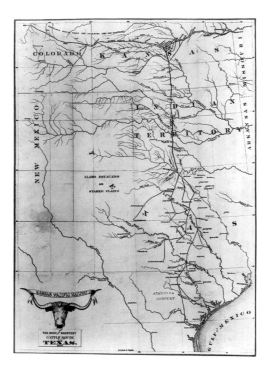

The Great Texas Cattle Trail is portrayed as the "best and shortest" route from Texas to Kansas on this nineteenth-century promotional map. Published in 1872 by the Kansas Pacific Railway, the map and accompanying guide book were intended for "gratuitous distribution." (*Titled Collection*)

a researcher may find filed next to valuable original printed maps photocopies of important maps from libraries in the United States, England, France, Italy, or Spain.

Maps of the United States are housed in more than seven thousand drawers of the Titled Collection. Here is found a record of the small towns and large cities, states and regions, and the country as a whole. Included are the full range of cartographic materials, from general purpose maps to thematic maps in nearly five hundred categories. Many of the pre-1900 maps of the United States are described in *Maps of America* (Washington, 1901), compiled by Philip Lee Phillips. While selected card files and specialized bibliographies of states or cities have supplanted this volume for some areas, it is still the best record of the voluminous file of early maps showing the entire United States or its major regions.

Early general maps of the United States are housed in approximately eighty drawers, among which are many editions of desk-size and wall-size maps by such prominent American cartographers as John Melish, Henry S. Tanner, G. Woolworth Colton, S. Augustus Mitchell, David Burr, John Disturnell, H. H. Lloyd, and Gaylord Watson. This part of the collection is most extensive for the midpart of the nineteenth century when the rapid expansion of the United States gave cause for the publication of many significant wall-size maps of the nation, such as the many editions of the "official" map of the country published by the General Land Office.

Beginning in the 1850s, entrepreneurs initiated an important phase in the history of American cartography by producing very detailed maps of counties. Often called "land ownership maps" because they indicate the farms and residences of subscribers, these were usually the first maps of most counties in the Northeast and Midwest, and the Great Plains states. In addition to showing land owners throughout the county, they often contain inset maps of towns and villages as well as vignettes of residences, businesses, and farms. County land ownership maps are among the most heavily used materials in the division because of their value to genealogical studies. The Titled Collection contains nearly fifteen hundred such maps published before 1900, which are described in *Land Ownership Maps: A Checklist of Nineteenth-Century United States County Maps in the Library of Congress* (Washington, 1967). Before the end of the nineteenth century, most publishers had abandoned the wall map format in favor of county atlases. A few firms continued producing county land ownership maps, although in a less elaborate style, well into the twentieth century.

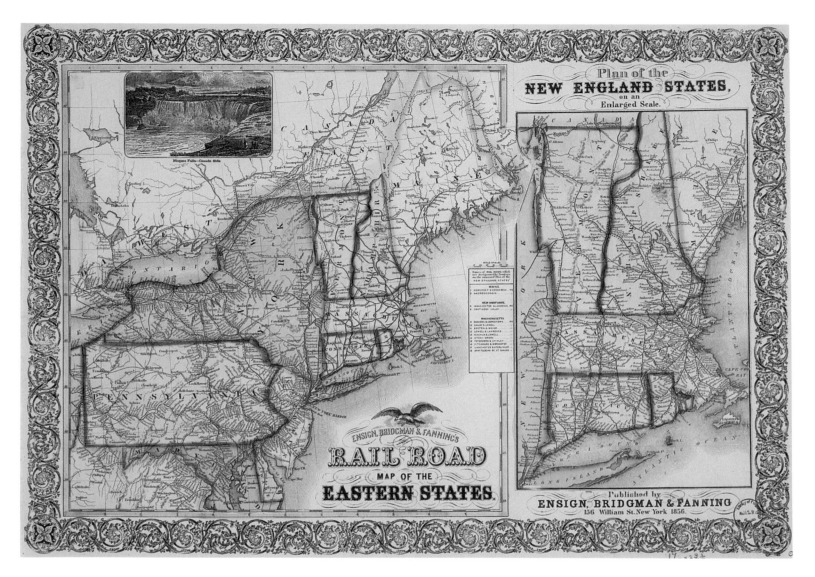

Railroad maps constitute another important group of maps relating to the growth of the United States. Several hundred of these maps, which are described in *Railroad Maps of the United States* (Washington, 1975), are found in the Titled Collection, where they are organized into three categories: those showing the rail network of the whole country, an individual state, or a single railroad company. A selection of these maps is also featured in another Library of Congress publication, *Railroad Maps of North America: The First Hundred Years* (Washington, 1984).

Road maps are also well represented in the Titled Collection. With the

Published by Ensign, Bridgman & Fanning in New York City in 1856, this map documents the developing railroad network in the Middle Atlantic and New England states before the Civil War. The growing urbanization and industrialization of this region depended on the rapid construction of an integrated transportation system. *(Titled Collection)*

development of the automobile and the national system of highways, the road map was created to meet the needs of early automobile enthusiasts. The division's collection of American road maps, for both the nation and individual states, documents the evolution of this particular form of cartography and captures more clearly than any other medium the development of a transportation system oriented to individual movement.

A special strength of the Titled Collection is the wealth of American city plans, particularly for the major urban centers of the nation. In terms of volume, there are eight cities for which there are exceptionally large holdings: Boston (45 drawers), New York (100 drawers), Philadelphia (43 drawers), Washington, D.C. (114 drawers), Detroit (21 drawers), Chicago (42 drawers), Los Angeles (37 drawers), and San Francisco (25 drawers). The maps in these drawers range from basic street plans to special purpose maps. The maps of Detroit are described in *Detroit and Vicinity Before 1900* (Washington, 1968), while ward maps for thirty-five cities are listed in *Ward Maps of United States Cities* (Washington, 1975).

There is less bibliographic description for single-sheet maps of the rest of the world. *Maps of America* lists many pretwentieth-century maps of the Caribbean, Central America, and South America, and *Selected Maps and Charts of Antarctica* (Washington, 1959) describes single-sheet maps of Antarctica published from 1945 to 1959, a period in which there were numerous large government scientific expeditions sent to that continent. As might be expected, the contents of this portion of the Titled Collection reflects best those areas where cartography developed into an important discipline. Canada and the European nations (especially the United Kingdom, Germany, and France) are well represented in the collections for both historic and current materials. Portions of the world that became parts of European empires were also well mapped in the latter part of the nineteenth century and the early twentieth century.

Relative sizes of different portions of the collection can be inferred from drawer counts: Mexico (190 drawers), Central America (360 drawers), South America (695 drawers), Europe (4,360 drawers), Asia (1,350 drawers), Africa (635 drawers), and Australia, New Zealand, and Oceania (480 drawers). Notable countries, in terms of size of the collection, include: Germany (765 drawers), France (720 drawers), Japan (300 drawers), United Kingdom (275 drawers), the former USSR (200 drawers, in addition to 64 drawers of city maps that have been cataloged), and China (110 drawers).

An extremely important segment of this part of the collection are the 210 drawers of world maps. Approximately 40 percent of these are general reference

OPPOSITE: The widespread use of the automobile during the first half of the twentieth century saw the proliferation of inexpensive road maps, several of which are illustrated here. Some, such as the "Shell Road Map of Pennsylvania," which was published in 1933 by The H. M. Gousha Company, were distributed free by the gas companies, while others, such as the "Official Auto Trails Map," which was published by Rand McNally in 1922, were sold at relatively low prices. *(Titled Collection)*

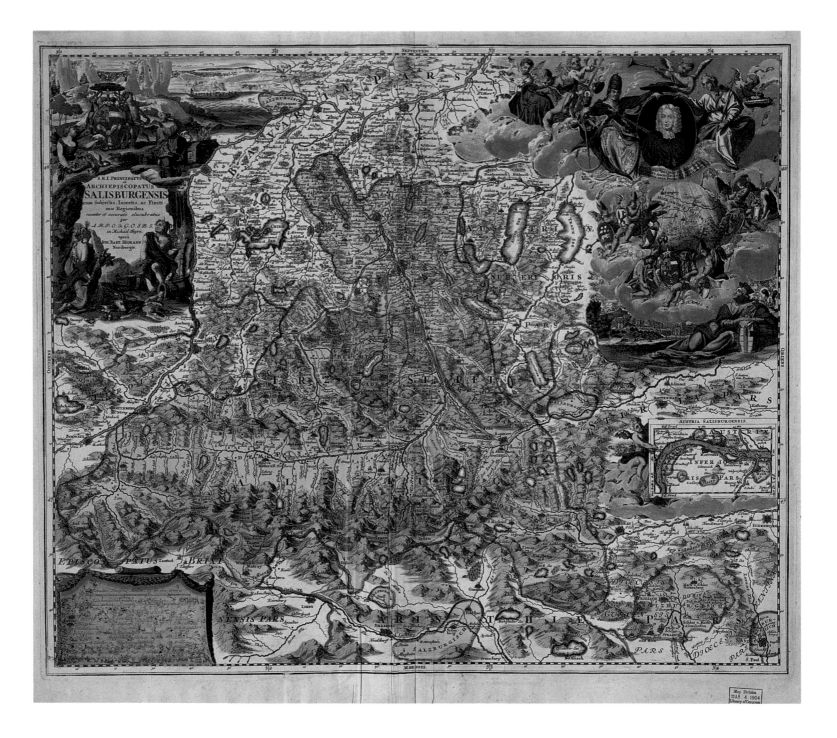

maps that are arranged chronologically. In addition to original printed maps, there are many facsimiles and photocopies of important world maps from archives and libraries elsewhere in this country and Europe that record the growing geographical knowledge of the earth gained from the European discoveries and exploration that began during the Renaissance. The remainder of the world maps are organized by a variety of subjects, thirty-five of which have at least one or more drawers of maps.

Nineteenth-century maps for virtually all European nations are consulted in part to determine changing political boundaries and to find the location of villages and towns from which ancestors emigrated. In recent years, limited access to the resources of countries under Soviet domination made the division's collections the primary source of cartographic information about those nations.

Military and ethnographic maps constitute heavily used categories of the European portions of the Titled Collection. In particular, there are exceptionally strong holdings for maps from the Napoleonic Wars and the first and second world wars. In recent years, considerable research regarding the Holocaust has been conducted within these categories, with emphasis on the location of towns, the movement of peoples throughout Europe, journalistic and propaganda use of maps, and the location of concentration camps. Many maps showing the distribution of various ethnic groups within individual countries were prepared after World War I, as the peacemakers attempted to redraw political boundaries that more closely approximated ethnic boundaries.

Outside the European area, holdings are not nearly as extensive. An important portion of the collection, however, is the grouping labelled Bible Lands, consisting of seventeen drawers of historical maps. They emphasize such Old Testament themes as Canaan, Exodus, Patriarchs, Judges, and Kings, while New Testament themes include the Birth and Life of Christ, Apostles, and Paul.

Much of the early mapping of Asian and African countries was conducted by European colonial governments. Consequently, the collections are very rich in the portrayal of colonial place names and boundaries as well as the cities established as administrative and commercial centers. There are extensive files of city plans for many of the major urban centers of the world. The great European cities, such as London, Paris, Berlin, and Rome, are well represented over the course of several centuries. For the Western Hemisphere, Mexico City, Quebec, and Montreal

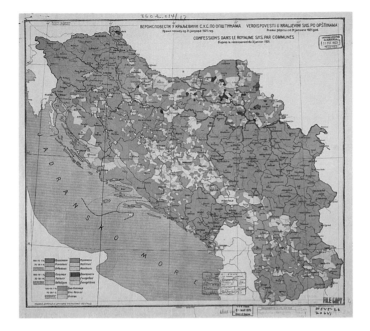

ABOVE. After World War I, ethnographic and cultural maps were prepared of the various European countries as part of the process of drawing new political boundaries. Based on 1921 data, this map shows the distribution of the four dominant religions (Orthodox, Muslim, Catholic, and Protestant) in the former Kingdom of the Serbs, Croats, and Slovenes, which until its breakup in the *early* 1990s was known as Yugoslavia. (*Titled Collection*)

OPPOSITE: Representative of richly decorated eighteenth-century maps prepared for the European map trade, this map depicts the Salzburg province in Austria. It was compiled by the German publisher Johann Baptist Homann. (*Titled Collection*)

have the largest number of maps. For many cities, maps from this century are in more demand for research than the earlier ones. This is particularly true for the major Chinese cities of Shanghai and Canton, the maps of which are frequently consulted in the division's reading room.

MULTI-SHEET MAP SERIES

Map series, consisting of multiple sheets of maps published at a uniform size and utilizing standardized symbols, include approximately two million map sheets in 12,000 series, constituting the largest and most comprehensive collection of medium- and large-scale map series ever assembled. Virtually every major national mapping organization is represented. These series encompass such diverse subjects as general topographic maps; thematic maps depicting special subjects such as geology, landuse, and census data; large-scale plans of cities; transportation maps; aeronautical charts; and hydrographic charts.

The geographical coverage dates from the beginning of large-scale topographic mapping and nautical charting in the eighteenth century. Series produced before 1900 focus more heavily on Western Europe, reflecting the longer tradition of large-scale mapping in this region. Series produced during the first half of the twentieth century provide good coverage for Europe, East Asia, and portions of Africa since these regions were heavily mapped by competing armies or colonial powers. With the end of the Cold War, the division has once again begun acquiring current, large-scale topographic series of Eastern Europe and the former Soviet Union. Because of the time and cost of surveying large areas at a detailed scale, most of the map series were produced by official mapping organizations.

The collection has been developed primarily through the deposit of new issues and reprints of standard map and chart series produced by official mapping and charting agencies and also through the transfer of obsolete and superceded materials from federal map libraries, particularly the former Army Map Service (AMS) Library and its successor, the Defense Mapping Agency Hydrographic/ Topographic Center Library. International exchanges and purchases coordinated by an interagency procurement committee directed by the State Department, a program that dates from 1948, have also been a major source of maps.

The earliest multisheet map series is the *Carte géométrique de la France*, or more commonly, *Carte de Cassini*, completed by César François Cassini de Thury and his son Jacques-Dominique in 1789 (180 sheets at the scale of 1:86,400). The first general topographic map of the an entire country based on a network of

OPPOSITE: Paris and its neighboring villages and forests are the focus of the "first sheet" of the *Carte géométrique de la France*. Completed in 1789, this was the first multisheet, topographic map series of an entire country. (*Map Series Collection*)

meticulously surveyed triangles, the *Carte de Cassini* established the basic principles of national mapping which are still employed throughout the world today. A year later the British Ordnance Survey was established to prepare a topographic map of England and Ireland for military and administrative purposes. Similar national surveys were soon begun in other European countries, all of which are found in the Library's collection.

European colonial powers were the first to undertake large-scale topographic surveys in other parts of the world. The British established the Survey of India in 1767 but it was not until 1802 that a geodetic triangulation of the subcontinent was begun and the first period of topographic surveys initiated. The Dutch Topographic Service began mapping in the Netherlands East Indies (Indonesia) in the 1860s. Similarly, the first official topographic maps of Cambodia, Laos, and Vietnam were prepared by the French Army's Topographic Bureau in 1886. Most other national topographic mapping programs were created in the twentieth century. For historical research, these series are especially valuable because individual sheets were revised periodically to reflect internal improvements such as canals, roads, and railroads, growth of urban areas, and boundary and name changes.

Large-scale map series of Central and East European countries are among the most frequently consulted maps in the collections because of their value to genealogists attempting to locate the names of towns from which their ancestors emigrated. The *Karte des Deutschen Reiches*, for example, consists of 674 separate map sheets. Most of these sheets were revised one or more times resulting in a total count of 4,074 map sheets covering the period from 1879 to 1944. Printed at a scale of 1:100,000 by the German mapping organization Riechsamt für Landesaufnahme, this series provides geographic coverage for pre-World War II Germany, which included parts of present-day Poland and Russia.

The division has a nearly complete set of the various series of topographic maps of the United States issued by the U.S. Geological Survey. The most detailed current topographic maps are at the scale of 1:24,000 for forty-nine states and 1:63,360 for Alaska.

Series at 1:100,000 and 1:250,000 are complete for the country.

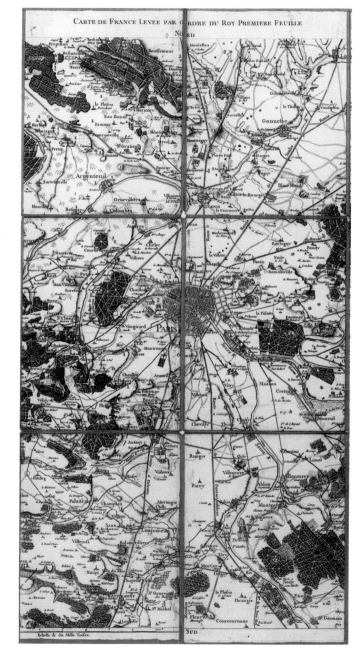

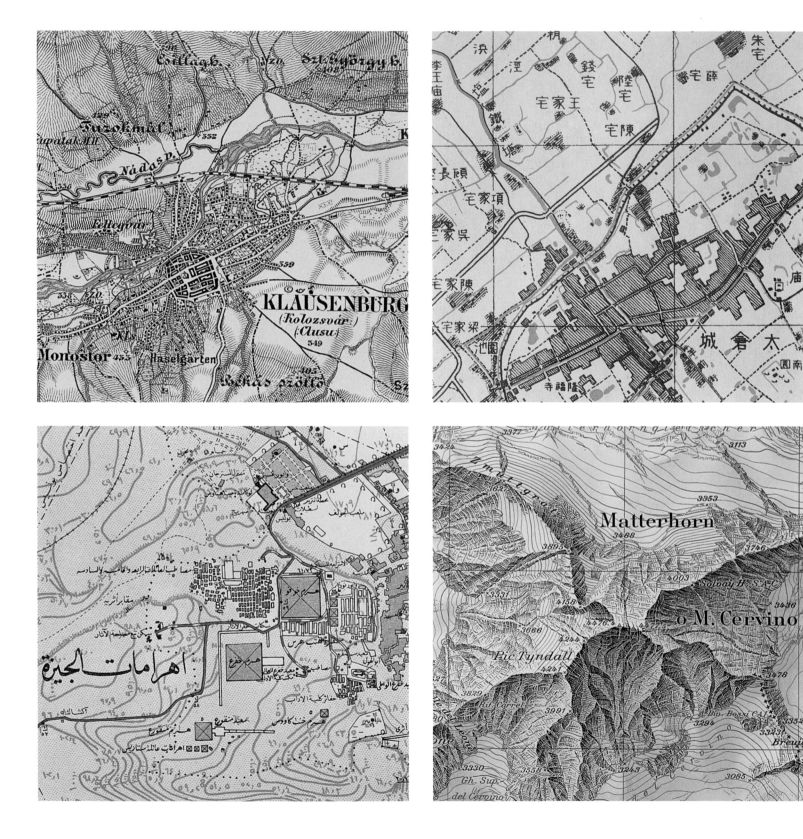

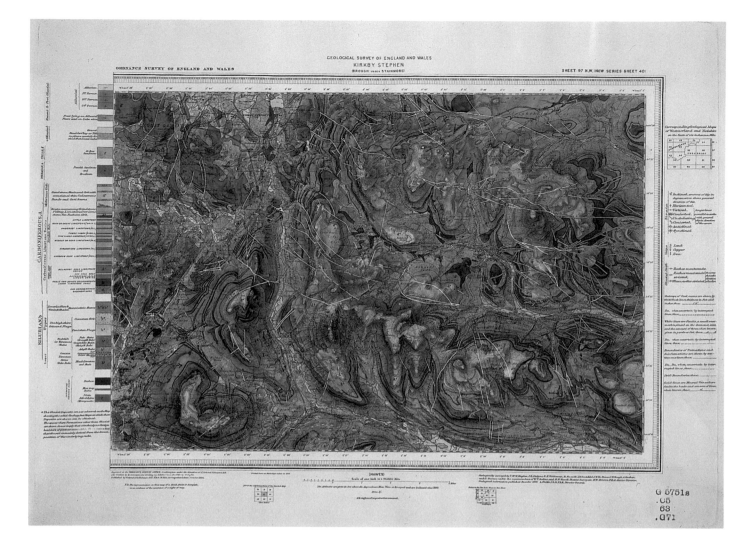

Representative selection of large-scale, multisheet series maps issued by official government mapping organizations: (OPPOSITE TOP LEFT) A detail of a topographic map (1/75,000) of Austria-Hungary, by the Austro-Hungarian Militargeographische Institut, showing the city of Cluj in Romania, also known as Klausenberg in German and Kolozsvar in Hungarian, in 1875.
(OPPOSITE TOP RIGHT) A detail of a planimetric map (1/25,000) of China, by the Japanese Expeditionary Forces in Shanghai, showing a walled Chinese city and irrigation system in 1932.
(OPPOSITE BOTTOM LEFT) A detail of a topographic map (1/25,000) of Egypt, by the Survey of Egypt, showing the Giza Pyramids along the Nile River in northern Egypt in 1932.
(OPPOSITE BOTTOM RIGHT) A detail of a topographic map (1/25,000) of Switzerland, by the Swiss Bundesamt für Landestopographie, showing the rugged relief of the Matterhorn in 1991. *(Map Series Collection)*

ABOVE: This hand-colored geological sheet was issued by the Geological Survey of England and Wales, the first national geological survey organization. It portrays the geological structure in an area on the border of Westmoreland and Yorkshire in 1889. *(Map Series Collection)*

There are also historic series dating from the 1880s at scales of 1:62,500, 1:125,000, and 1:250,000.

Topographic surveys are valuable in part because they serve as a framework on which other information can be mapped. Geological information, in particular, is best understood when presented in relation to surface topography. The multi-sheet map collection is particularly strong with respect to geological maps. The earliest represented is the geologic survey of Saxony, begun in 1830 under the direction of Carl Friedrich Nauman and Carl Bernhard von Cotta, geologists associated with the famed mining academy in Freiberg. The Library also has extensive holdings of the Geological Survey of England and Wales, the first national geological survey which began in 1835 with the appointment of Henry de la Beche, an English stratigrapher and structural geologist. Since color is crucial to the portrayal of geological information, these early maps were meticulously hand colored with as many as seventy different tints displayed to distinguish different rock units.

Other multi-sheet maps focus on such special subjects as vegetation, forestry, soils, demography, and topics relating to environmental issues. For example, the U.S. Fish and Wildlife Service recently deposited a set of almost nineteen thousand National Wetland Inventory maps that were prepared as the result of a 1986 Congressional action to aid industry, agriculture and government decisionmaking on this subject.

The development of national mapping programs in the nineteenth century laid the foundation for multiple sheet series at various scales designed specifically for artillery and tactical use. For World War I, the collections include extensive series of French, British, German, and American maps at scales as large as 1:10,000 and 1:20,000 showing networks of trenches and positions of artillery units. Following the war, a special series of French maps was prepared to show the devastated regions.

A large number of the multi-sheet map series were also produced during World War II. All of the major military belligerents devoted extensive resources to compiling maps. The primary topographic map-producing organizations for the Allies were the British Directorate of Military Survey, War Office, Geographical Section, General Staff (GSGS), and the U. S. Army Map Service (AMS). In an unprecedented example of cooperation, Great Britain assumed primary responsibility for mapping the Eastern Hemisphere while the United States focused on the Western Hemisphere and the western Pacific. Their combined production totaled more than one billion printed sheets covering most of Europe, North Africa, and East and South Asia. Following World War II, the Library acquired a considerable number of German and Japanese military multi-sheet maps captured by

OPPOSITE: An early experimental air navigation strip map produced by the Air Service of the U.S. Army in 1923 shows insets of individual landing fields in red and prominent features along an air route from New York City to Bellefonte, Pennsylvania. (*Map Series Collection*)

American military units, particularly maps of Europe produced by the German Generalstab des Heeres (General Staff of the Army) and of northern and eastern China and Manchuria surveyed by the Japanese Kwantung Army, the Japanese General Staff, and the Japanese Imperial Survey during the 1930s. Among the captured maps are tactical and operational map series produced by the Soviet General'nyy Shtab Krasnoy Armii (General Staff of the Red Army), the Glavnoye Upravleniye Geodezii i Kartografii (GUGK), and the Narodyy Komissariat Vnutrennykh Del (NKVD) which had been initially captured by German forces, including some which contain German military maps printed on the verso.

Military map series prepared for American units in Korea and Vietnam are also housed in the division. The 1:50,000 scale maps for Vietnam (L7014 series) prepared by the Defense Mapping Agency (DMA) are available for reference use but most large-scale military maps are restricted to official use. This restriction also applies to other DMA topographic series covering selected Third World countries.

The fall of the iron curtain and the liberalization of the former communist countries of Eastern Europe and Russia has provided a new opportunity to build upon the division's existing strong collection of early large-scale topographic maps of these countries. Since 1990 the Geography and Map Division has devoted considerable attention to acquiring cartographic resources from this region and other geographic areas where map distribution had been restricted. Through purchases, transfers, gifts, and exchange agreements, the Library of Congress has begun to fill a fifty-year gap in its international holdings. Recent detailed cartographic coverage has been acquired for Albania, Poland, Hungary, the Czech Republic, Slovakia, Bulgaria, the former Soviet Union, and the former Yugoslavia. Of special interest is the recent acquisition of large-scale coverage of Soviet mapping of London, Stockholm, Rotterdam, and forty-seven other cities.

The twentieth century saw the development of the aeronautical chart. In the early years of aviation, there were few navigational aids, and pilots used physical features on the ground as landmarks along their route. The earliest example of this type in the division is a series of *Carte aéronautique* issued by the French Service Géographique de l'Armée about 1911. About the same time, the Aéro-Club de France began issuing a series of "strip charts," narrow maps that showed the area along common flight paths. During World War I, the *Carte de l'Aéro Club de France* provided the primary aeronautical charts used on the Western Front.

In the United States, the U.S. Army Air Service began the production of air navigation strip maps in 1923 that showed prominent features along Army air routes between principal cities, and a year later the U.S. Hydrographic Office

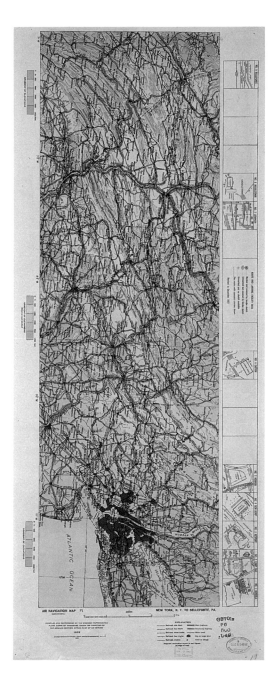

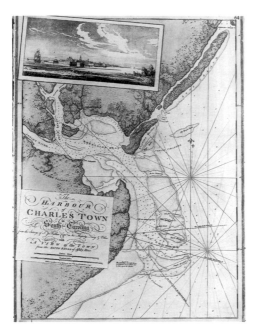

This chart of Charleston, South Carolina, harbor is from the *Atlantic Neptune*, a collection of charts based on the first systematic survey of the American coast. Published between 1774 and 1781, the *Atlantic Neptune* was prepared by Joseph Frederick Wallet des Barres for the British Admiralty. (Atlantic Neptune *Collection*)

issued aviation charts of coastal areas. Following the passage of the Air Commerce Act in 1926, the Commerce Department's Coast and Geodetic Survey began compiling airway strip maps that provided coverage for an emerging civilian air industry and shortly thereafter introduced a standardized series of charts that covered the whole nation. The coverage of air navigation charts expanded dramatically during World War II with charts produced by all of the major air forces being well represented.

The development of cartography during and after the Renaissance was closely intertwined with nautical charting; subsequently, modern hydrographic surveying has become a highly specialized and separate discipline. A major component of the Division's multi-sheet map series is the official nautical charts produced by fifty-five nations. New charts and editions contribute to the steady stream of new receipts each year. The entire history of nautical charting is well represented in the collections.

The beginning of organized hydrographic surveying and chart production at a national level can also be traced to France with the founding of Le Depôt des Cartes et Plans de la Marine in 1720, shortly before César François Cassini de Thury began his work on the first national topographic map. Jacques Nicolas Bellin, the Royal Hydrographer and head of the agency, initiated a number of hydrographic atlases in the mid-1700s that covered the coasts of France as well as the rest of the world. In the mid-1830s, Adm. Jacques Hamelin, Director of the Depôt from 1832 until 1839, presented to the Naval Observatory in Washington, the predecessor of the U.S. Navy's Hydrographic Office, a set of French nautical charts bound in thirty-nine volumes that were subsequently transferred to the Library of Congress. The division's collection of loose-sheet, French nautical charts is housed in nearly one hundred drawers, containing approximately twenty thousand charts.

The British Admiralty's organized hydrographic activities date from 1795, with the appointment of Alexander Dalrymple to the position of Royal Hydrographer. Dalrymple, who had achieved considerable knowledge and expertise as the hydrographer for the East India Company, assembled several compilations of charts dating from 1703 to 1807, which are included in the division's atlas collection. After the appointment of Francis Beaufort to the position of hydrographer in 1829, the British Admiralty became the dominant charting organization in the world. The division's collection of loose-sheet British Admiralty charts, dating from the mid-1800s, is housed in approximately 350 drawers and contains an estimated 35,000 sheets.

The 1816 appointment of Ferdinand Hassler, a Swiss mathematician and surveyor, to head the U.S. Coast Survey, which had been established in 1807 by Thomas

Jefferson, marked the beginning of significant charting activity in this country. Although its responsibilities have been expanded to include the maintenance of the nation's infrastructure of geodetic control stations and the production of aeronautical charts, the agency is still producing nautical charts of the United States under the name of the U.S. Coast and Geodetic Survey. As the country expanded, the Coast Survey extended its operations first from the Atlantic to the Gulf Coast, then to the Pacific waters of California, Oregon, and Washington, to Alaska, and finally to Hawaii and other islands in the Pacific. The division's holdings of Coast Survey charts include a collection housed in 250 drawers, containing an estimated 25,000 sheets.

As the U.S. Navy expanded its activities around the world in the early 1800s to provide protection for the nation's expanding maritime commerce, the Hydrographic Office was organized within the Navy Department to supervise the surveying and charting of foreign waters. This operation initially formed within the Naval Observatory, known as the Depot of Charts, under the direction of Lt. Charles Wilkes. After just a few years in this position, Wilkes left to head the U.S. Exploring Expedition in the years 1837 to 1842. The charts produced during that voyage to Antarctica, the Tuamotu Archipelago and the Society Islands, the Fiji and Samoa Groups, Hawaii, and the Northwest Coast of America were first published as a separate atlas but subsequently were used as the core material around which charting of foreign waters was developed. Wilkes's successor at the Depot of Charts, Lt. Matthew Fontaine Maury, was instrumental in expanding the production of charts. For nearly one hundred forty years the Hydrographic Office operated as a separate entity, and the total production of the agency is represented by a collection of 170 drawers with approximately 17,000 sheets.

In addition to the charts of the United States, Great Britain, and France, the division has important historical charts from other countries, including Argentina, Australia, Japan, Germany, Latvia, Mexico, Spain, Russia, and the former Yugoslavia. A large number of captured Japanese and German charts were transferred to the division after World War II. Charts from this era reflect the fact that even after a century of organized chart making, the world's waters were still imperfectly known. The Japanese and American charts of Tarawa, for example, one of the costliest World War II invasions by U.S. Marines in the Pacific, were based on a survey made by the U.S. Exploring Expedition in 1841 and updated with just minor corrections by the British Admiralty in 1925!

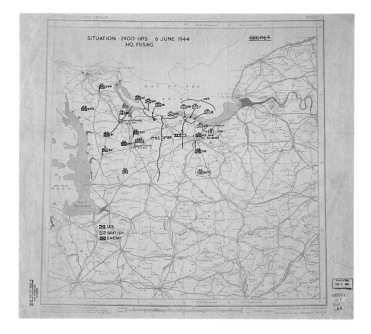

Daily situation maps prepared by the 12th Army Group of the European Allied Forces record the liberation of France starting with the invasion of Normandy on D-Day, June 6, 1944. This multisheet series shows the location of the 12th Army Group and adjacent Allied forces as well as the German units for each day until July 26, 1945. (*Map Series Collection*)

Globes and Terrain Models

OPPOSITE: A small manuscript terrestrial globe housed within a series of eleven interlocking armillary rings is the division's oldest globe. It was produced in 1543 by the Cologne mathematician and geographer, Caspar Vopell. *(Globe Collection)*

MINIATURE REPRESENTATIONS of the earth in the form of globes and terrain models have a long history, and are well represented in the collections by more than three hundred terrestrial and celestial globes, armillary spheres, one hundred fifty globe gores (the paper segments used in the construction of globes), illustrations of globes, and treatises on globe construction and use. Globes come in a wide variety of sizes and formats, including pocket globes which were usually enclosed in fish-skin cases, inflatable globes, dissected globes, and folded items such as R. Buckminster Fuller's "Dymaxion Globe."

The earliest surviving globes were produced in Germany. The division recently acquired an exact facsimile of the oldest extant European globe, which was made by Martin Behaim of Nuremberg in 1492. Germany was also the site of the construction of the division's rarest globe, which was produced in 1543 by the Cologne mathematician and geographer, Caspar Vopell. It consists of a small manuscript terrestrial globe housed within a series of eleven interlocking armillary rings which illustrates the rotation of the sun, moon, and stars in the Ptolemaic tradition.

In 1984 the Library purchased a pair of large, rare terrestrial and celestial globes constructed in 1688 and 1693, respectively, by the famed Venetian cosmographer and globe maker, Vincenzo Coronelli. Each measures 110 centimeters in diameter and stands nearly two meters high on heavy mahogany stands. This terrestrial globe is noted for depicting California as an island. Extremely rare (the only complete pair of Coronelli globes in North America), the globes are currently on public display on the sixth floor of the Madison Building. The Library of Congress also owns a copy of Coronelli's 1696 eighteen-inch terrestrial globe (which was presented to William III) and a copy of his extremely rare *Libro dei Globi*, an atlas which includes all the globe gores published by Coronelli.

In addition to these rarities, the Library's collections include a matched pair of nine-inch terrestrial and celestial globes by the renowned Dutch map maker, Jodocus Hondius, constructed in Milan in 1615 by Joseph di Rossi; a pair of twelve-inch celestial and terrestrial globes produced in 1816 by the London map maker, Matthew Cary; a twenty-centimeter globe by Johann Doppelmayr dated 1750; and a seven-centimeter pocket globe by John Senex produced circa 1730.

Globes were widely used as educational tools in nineteenth-century America and were more popular than their current representation in American museums and libraries would suggest. During the past decade, the Geography and Map Division has made a concerted effort to assemble a strong collection of globes produced by American manufacturers. Through a combination of gifts and purchases, twenty-five globes from the estate of Howard E. Welsh, the preeminent

collector of American globes, was acquired in 1991. With these additions, the division now holds the major study collection for globes produced in the United States.

America's first commercial globe maker, James Wilson (1763–1855), who was largely self-taught in geography and the techniques of engraving and globe construction, constructed his first globe in 1810, determined to produce globes that equaled those then being imported from England. The Library holds a copy of his second published work, a thirteen-inch terrestrial globe constructed in 1811, three variant copies of his three-inch globes, and six of his thirteen-inch terrestrial and celestial globes. Other leading early American globe makers whose works are found in the collections include A. H. Andrews & Co., Silas Cornell, Brown and Peirce, Josiah Holbrook, Gilman Joslyn, Josiah Loring, David C. Murdock, and John B. Pendleton.

During most of the division's history, the acquisition of globes and globe gores depended primarily upon copyright deposits; therefore, the collection is particularly strong for late-nineteenth- and twentieth-century globes and globe gores produced by major U.S. publishing houses such as Weber Costello, Cram, National Geographic Society, Rand McNally, and Replogle.

In addition to the two large Coronelli globes, the division has three other custom-made, floor-mounted showcase globes. The first, which is known as the "President's Globe," is a fifty-inch sphere that was designed and compiled by the Office of Strategic Services during World War II for use by Allied war leaders. Manufactured by the Weber-Costello Company in Chicago in 1942, one copy was presented to Pres. Franklin D. Roosevelt in December of that year and another to Sir Winston Churchill. Copies were also displayed in the House and Senate Chambers in the U.S. Capitol. The globe, formerly in the House of Representatives, was transferred to the Library of Congress on October 15, 1946.

The second showcase model is a seventy-four-inch replica of planet Earth which was received in 1980 on loan from the National Archives. One of eight globes designed and constructed by Terr-a-qua Globes and Maps, Incorporated between 1966 and 1973, the illuminated globe depicts in raised relief all three surface features—ocean floor, ocean surface, and continental topography . Originally presented to the National Archives by the Talbert and Leota Abrams Foundation in honor of Antarctic explorers Capt. and Mrs. Finn Ronne, the globe is on display at the entrance to the Geography and Map Division. The division's third large floor-mounted globe was presented to the Library in 1992 by Andrew McNally III, chairman of the Rand McNally Company, to commemorate the Columbus Quincentenary and the Twenty-seventh International

Geographical Congress. This hand-painted geophysical globe is on permanent display on the second floor of the Madison Building.

Another cartographic device used to represent or model portions of the Earth's surface is the three-dimensional relief map, generally constructed for military or educational purposes from plaster, papier-mâché, sponge rubber, or vinyl plastic. The division holds four examples of relief maps constructed by native peoples, including replicas of ancient Polynesian stick charts constructed of a framework of coconut palm or pandanus reeds and cowrie shells designed to represent the patterns of ocean currents and the locations of atolls and islands.

The core of the division's terrain model map collections consists of some two thousand molded plastic relief quadrangle maps produced by the U.S. Army Map Service (AMS) at a horizontal scale of 1:250,000. First produced during the Korean War, AMS maps eventually expanded geographical coverage to include virtually all of Asia, Europe, and North America. Although more than two million plastic relief reproductions were produced from the 2,000 master molds from 1951 to the 1970s, the division's collection is the only known complete collection available for study in a public facility.

Terrain models were used extensively by military forces during World War II. Although thousands were produced in portable workshops behind front lines, aboard warships, and in permanent establishments in Pearl Harbor, London, and Washington, D.C., few have survived. Fortunately for researchers, the division has several examples. These include models of Bangkok, Hong Kong, and two Pacific islands prepared by Navy terrain model units in Pearl Harbor and Washington, D. C., from 1944 to 1945. Constructed with the aid of aerial photographs and reconnaissance reports, these models were cast in rubber for use in amphibious operations. Complementing this material is a large relief map of the Soviet Union in three sections and a three-dimensional prototype globe fabricated and donated by Leonard N. Abrams, a skilled globe and model maker who began his career as a terrain modeler with the Army Map Service during World War II.

In addition, the division holds a study collection of 300 commercial terrain models produced in the United States and Europe from the 1890s to the present. Many were constructed for use in school classrooms, for business and industry boardrooms, and for wall decorations in private homes. Models are still an important cartographic format, as demonstrated by a solid plastic tactile relief model in three sections of Capitol Hill and the Mall in Washington, D.C., sponsored by Congress in 1988, for the use of the blind and visually handicapped.

ABOVE: An unusual example of a three-dimensional model is this map of the Crown Prince Islands in Disco Bay on the west coast of Greenland that was constructed with sealskin and driftwood by Silas Sandgreen, an Eskimo hunter. The map was commissioned by the Library of Congress in 1925 through the efforts of the Secretary of the Navy, Admr. Richard E. Byrd, the noted Arctic and Antarctic explorer, and the Danish government. (*Vault Map Collection*)

OPPOSITE: The zodiacal constellations of Gemini, Cancer, and Leo are illustrated on these two globe gores from the 1615 celestial globe issued by the Dutch map maker Jodocus Hondius. (*Globe Collection*)

AERIAL SURVEY
MANHATTAN ISLAND, New York City
Made by
FAIRCHILD AERIAL CAMERA CORPORATION
New York City, August 4, 1921
This Mosaic was made by assembling 100 Aerial Photographs taken
while flying over the area at an altitude of 10,000 feet

Scale | 0   500   1000   1500   2000   2500   3000

Aerial Photographs and Remote Sensing Images

THE URGE TO VIEW the earth from above has deep historic roots. With the advent of human flight and the invention of photography, aerial images of the Earth's surface became an important tool in scientific, technical, and cartographic disciplines.

Aerial photographs, or printed versions known as photomaps, are found in many portions of the collections such as the Edgar Tobin Aerial Surveys Collection and the Nirenstein National Reality Company Collection. Many World War II era maps filed in the general collections are in the form of photomaps because they could be produced rapidly by tactical mapping units in the field to support military actions on the ground and for the identification of bombing targets.

The development of color photography and other specialized films expanded the range of applications to which aerial photography could be applied. In particular, the use of infrared film, which had a profound impact on the mapping of forests and crops, is well represented in the division's Remote Sensing Imagery and Aerial Photography Browse File. Aerial photography is such an important scientific tool that astronauts in virtually all of America's space programs have devoted time to taking hand-held photographs of the Earth. The division holds some 85,000 of these photographs on 16mm color film taken during Apollo, Gemini, Skylab, and Space Shuttle missions.

Just as the coincidental development of human flight and photography provided an impetus for change, the concurrent development of earth-orbiting satellites and computers marks another great milestone in cartographic history. Satellites provided a relatively inexpensive platform from which cameras could survey the earth on a regular basis. Computers and related technologies provided the foundation for a digital form of observation that eliminated the need for photographic film.

This revolutionary discipline was developed by the United States with the launching of the first Earth Resource Technology Satellite (later renamed Landsat) by NASA in 1972. Through the support of the U.S. Geological Survey and the National Oceanic and Atmospheric Administration in 1985, the division acquired approximately 650,000 16mm black-and-white photographic images of most countries generated from Landsat sensing devices at an altitude of some 570 miles. NASA also has deposited 630 eight- by ten-inch color photo images generated from Landsat satellites 1, 2, and 3 launched between 1972 and 1978. The photographs were selected by NASA scientists to illustrate significant geologic and topographic features and to demonstrate the value of Landsat imagery for scientific inquiry. Earth Observation Satellite Corporation, a private firm that currently manages

Landsat revealed whole new worlds hidden within the folds of a familiar world we thought we knew so well.

STEPHEN S. HALL
Mapping the Next Millennium, 1992

OPPOSITE: Detail of a photomosaic of Manhattan Island, New York, showing the lower portion of the island. Constructed from 100 aerial photographs taken by Fairchild Aerial Camera Corporation at an altitude of 1,000 feet on August 4, 1921, the photomosaic measures over eight feet in length. *(Vault Map Collection)*

RIGHT: Access to conventional black and white aerial photography is provided by microfiche copies of photomosaic indexes, such as this 1980 coverage of Carver County, Minnesota by the Agricultural Stabilization and Conservation Service. (*Remote Sensing and Aerial Photography Browse File*)

OPPOSITE: The confluence of the Rio Negro and the Amazon River in Brazil is shown on this Landsat image. Unlike a conventional photograph, this is a computer-generated image derived from reflected energy collected by a mapping satellite orbiting the earth at a distance of 438 miles. A false color image, the deep reds indicate the dense vegetation of the Amazon rain forests, while the lighter reds following the linear patterns of the road network reflect areas of deforestation. The heavily sedimented Rio Negro is shown in black while the Amazon appears in blue. (*Earth Observation Satellite Company Collection*)

the Landsat program for the federal government, recently donated a collection of 120 large format printed images generated from Landsat 4 and 5, representing many different areas of the world. A number of Landsat images produced by foreign organizations have also been acquired. The World Bank donated a set of nineteen satellite image maps of Nepal prepared by the Nepal National Remote Sensing Center in 1986.

Remote sensing will greatly alter the nature of cartography. Consequently, the Geography and Map Division will be collecting this new format of geographic information to complement the several centuries worth of traditional cartographic images of the earth that it holds. This new technology is highly dependent on powerful computers, and efforts are under way to provide the hardware and software necessary to use remotely sensed images of the earth. To date, the division has relied on collecting printed products derived from satellite imagery. Soon, however, government agencies and private firms will be releasing the digital forms of these images, and the division will begin collecting, cataloging, and servicing the actual data.

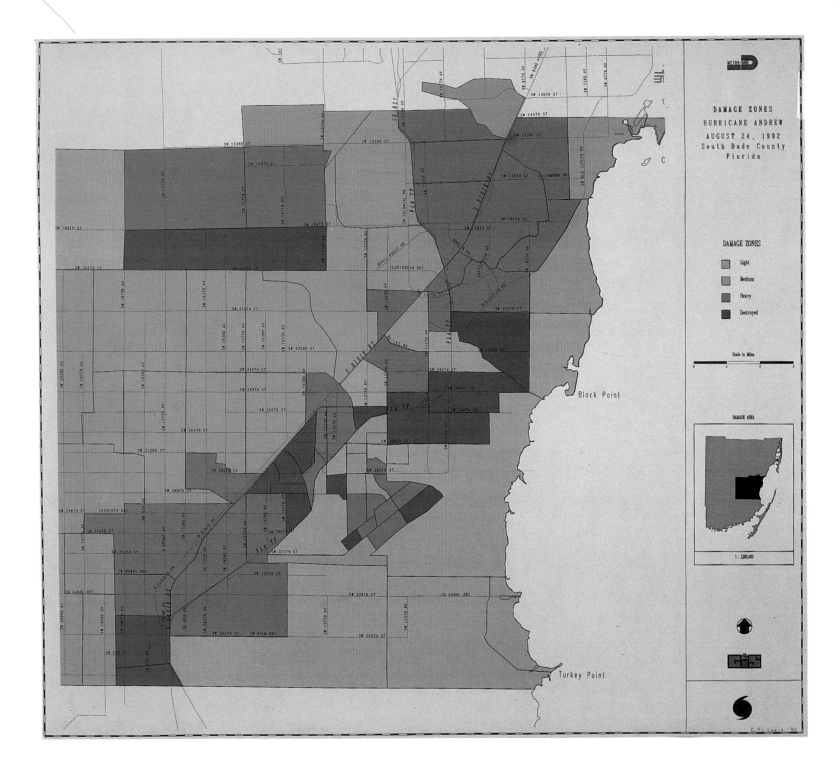

DAMAGE ZONES
HURRICANE ANDREW
AUGUST 24, 1992
South Dade County
Florida

DAMAGE ZONES

Light
Medium
Heavy
Destroyed

Scale in Miles

DAMAGE AREA

1 : 1,200,400

Black Point

Turkey Point

Digital Data and Geographic Information Systems

URING THE PAST DECADE, a revolution has drastically altered the nature of cartography. Beginning with efforts to automate merely the production of standard map products through the use of various computer technologies, a new industry evolved known as geographic information systems (GIS) that encompassed such processes as automated cartography, remote sensing from earth-orbiting satellites, and the sophisticated analysis of geographic information. Now the emphasis is on varied uses of geographic information in digital forms. In this environment, maps are frequently viewed as merely one of a wide variety of potential products. It is anticipated that by the turn of the century many of the products that are now published in paper form, such as topographic maps and nautical charts, will be produced electronically instead.

GIS treats data as different layers. For example, one layer may contain the street pattern of a city, another the administrative districts of the city, and a third might show the location of reported crimes. Within a GIS, the portrayal of each type of data can be tailored to meet specific criteria, and then the various layers combined to form a single map. One of the key features of a GIS is that any type of information with a geographic component can be mapped. Thus, thematic maps can be constructed from layers of data that represent traditional cartographic information and from data sets that the user supplies from other sources.

Some of the most important developments in GIS to date have come from the federal government. Probably the most significant is the *Topological Integrated Geographic Encoding Reference* (TIGER)/*Line Census File* developed for the 1990 census by the Bureau of the Census. The TIGER/*Line Census File* was created to describe the administrative units by which data for the 1990 decennial census would be collected and analyzed. It depicts most highways, railroads, streams, and administrative boundaries in the country. Because this file represents a basic seamless electronic map of the country, it has been adopted as the foundation of many GIS applications for such purposes as analyzing or controlling transportation, examining demographic patterns, or determining business locations. The TIGER/*Line Census File* is stored on forty-seven 3½-inch discs. Other major files include the U.S. Geological Survey Data Files and the U.S. National Cancer Institute Mapping Program.

Among the commercial software available are six packages produced by Environmental Systems Research Institute, Incorporated (ESRI), Redlands, California, which enable users to browse, query, and display thematic spatial data for the United States and the world at county, state, and country levels; and a package called *Marine Data Sampler*, designed to be used with ESRI's ArcView software; and

On a planet of finite resources faced with mounting population pressures, geographic information systems already have become indispensable for resource management, policy assessments, and strategic decisions.

CONGRESSMAN GEORGE E. BROWN
Chairman, House Science, Space, and Technology Committee quoted in *GISDEX Express,* 1992

OPPOSITE: Computer-generated map of Dade County, Florida, showing the extent of damage caused by Hurricane Andrew, August 22, 1992. This map was produced by Metro-Dade using *ArcView,* a sophisticated geographic information system developed by Environmental Systems Research Institute, Inc. (ESRI). (*Environmental Systems Research Institute, Inc. Collection*)

Magellan Geographix, a software and data set package on fifty-six 3½-inch discs that contains more than three hundred maps of cities, countries, regions, and continents, each of which can be displayed in multiple layers of some twenty existing attributes of information or new attributes which can be added by the operator.

Because the development of the GIS industry is in its formative stage and dominated by American firms, here and abroad, the Geography and Map Division is working to document its development. One of the pioneering firms, ESRI, has donated to the division the materials that have been exhibited at its Annual Users' Conference from 1982 to 1993. This is probably the single best collection of material which shows the ways in which GIS has developed as a discipline and has been applied to solving real world problems. It is hoped that collaboration with the GIS community will speed the Geography and Map Division along the path to the electronic era and also assist producers of GIS products and software to see the potential value of our historic materials to users of geographic information systems.

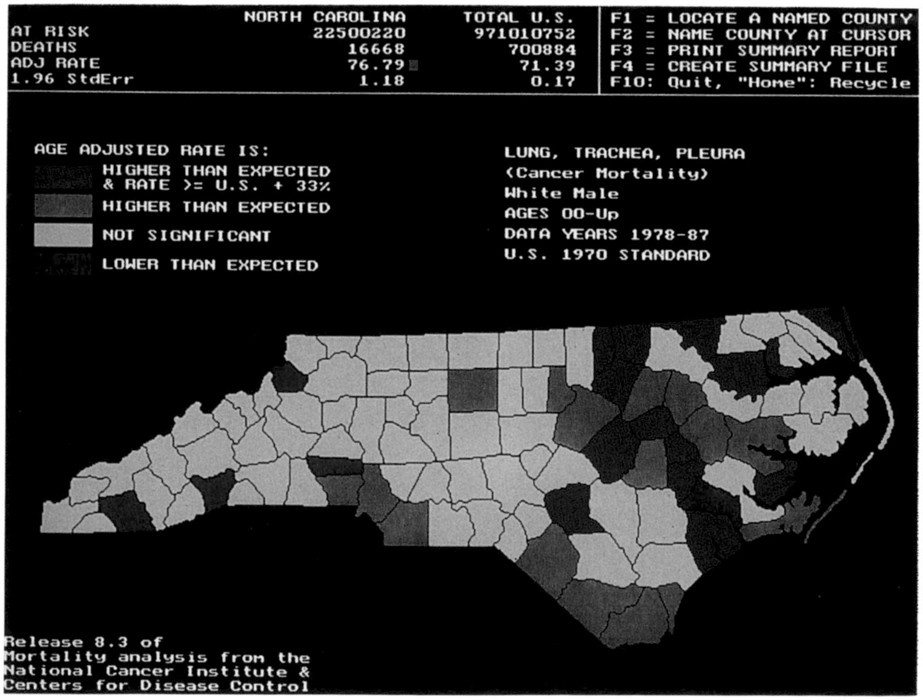

RIGHT: This computer-screen map, which shows mortality statistics for white males from lung, trachea, and pleura cancers in the state of North Carolina, is representative of the more than 100 million images that can be generated from the National Cancer Institute Mapping Program. This digital data base is stored on sixteen computer discs. (*U.S. National Cancer Institute Mapping Program*)

OPPOSITE: Political map of Europe showing national capitals and major cities as derived from *Magellan Geographix* digital map file. This image represents the base layers on which other layers of geographic information can be added. (*Magellan Geographix Database*)

	NORTH CAROLINA	TOTAL U.S.	F1 = LOCATE A NAMED COUNTY
AT RISK	22500220	971010752	F2 = NAME COUNTY AT CURSOR
DEATHS	16668	700884	F3 = PRINT SUMMARY REPORT
ADJ RATE	76.79	71.39	F4 = CREATE SUMMARY FILE
1.96 StdErr	1.18	0.17	F10: Quit, "Home": Recycle

AGE ADJUSTED RATE IS:

HIGHER THAN EXPECTED & RATE >= U.S. + 33%

HIGHER THAN EXPECTED

NOT SIGNIFICANT

LOWER THAN EXPECTED

LUNG, TRACHEA, PLEURA
(Cancer Mortality)
White Male
AGES 00-Up
DATA YEARS 1978-87
U.S. 1970 STANDARD

Release 8.3 of
Mortality analysis from the
National Cancer Institute &
Centers for Disease Control

Europe

⊛ National Capital
● Secondary City

Greenland (Denmark)

Greenland Sea

Arctic Circle

Jan Mayen (Norway)

Hammerfest

Narvik

Iceland
○ Reykjavik

Norwegian Sea

Sweden

Oulu

Umeå

Finland

Tampere

Helsinki

Russia

60°N

Faroe Islands (Denmark)

Troadheim

Norway

Bergen

Oslo

Gävle

Gulf of Finland

St. Petersburg

Shetland Islands

Stockholm

Tallinn

Estonia

Moscow

Orkney Islands

Skagerrak

Göteborg

Gotland

Riga

Atlantic

Hebrides

Aberdeen

North

Öland

Latvia

Edinburgh
Glascow

Denmark

Baltic Sea

Lithuania

Vilnius

Minsk

Oceaa

Newcastle

Sea

Copenhagen

Malmö

Bornholm

Russia

Gdansk

Belarus

50°

Belfast

Irish Sea

Liverpool

U.K.

Neth.

Rostock

Hamburg

Poznan

Warsaw

Kiyev (Kiev)

Ireland

Dublin

Cardiff

Amsterdam

Germany

Berlin

Poland

Krakow

L'vov

Ukraine

London

Brussels

Bonn

Prague

Czech Rep.

Slovakia

Belgium

Frankfurt

English Channel

Le Havre

Lux.

Luxembourg

Bratislava

Moldova

Kishinev

Odessa

Paris

Strasbourg

Munich

Danube

Vienna

Budapest

Hungary

Nantes

Switz.

Liech.

Austria

Romania

Black Sea

Bern

Slovenia

Ljubljana

Zagreb

Bucharest

Constanta

Bay of Biscac

France

Bordeaux

Milan

Venice

Croatia

Bos.& Herz.

Belgrade

Serbia

Bulgaria

Varna

Bilbao

San Marino

Adriatic Sea

Sarajevo

Sofia

Porto

Marseille

Monaco

Italy

Mont.

Podgorica

Skopje

Istanbul

Spain

Corsica

Rome

Tiranë

Mace.

Thessaloniki

Portugal

Barcelona

Alb.

Turkey

Lisbon

Madrid

Sardinia

Tyrrhenian Sea

Naples

Greece

Aegean Sea

Valencia

Balearic Islands

Ionian See

Pátrai

Athens

Málaga

Mediterranean Sea

Sicily

Crete

Rhodes

Strait of Gibraltaa

Gibraltar (U.K.)

Algiers

Tunis

Malta

Valletta

Morocco

Algeria

Tunisia

0   600 km

0   400

nautical miles

List of Special Collections

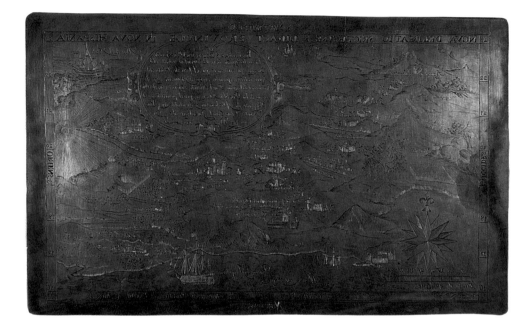

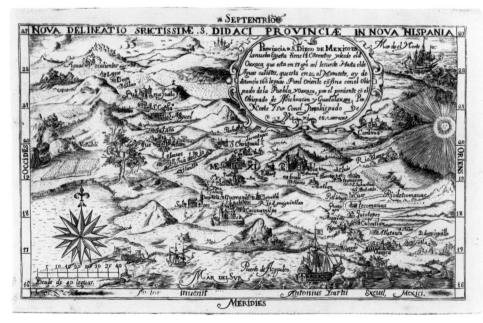

One of the earliest maps published in the New World was engraved on copper by Antonio Ysarti in Mexico City and printed by Juan de Ribero in 1682. Showing the Province of San Diego in New Spain, the engraving appeared in Balthassar de Medina's *Chronica de la Santa Provincia de San Diego de Mexico*. The Geography and Map Division holds both the original engraved copperplate and an impression taken from the plate. (*Printing Technology Collection*)

LEONARD N. ABRAMS GIFT (2 items). Hand-fabricated relief map of Soviet Union and prototype terrestrial globe.

ALGEMEEN RIJKSARCHIEF COLLECTION (1,519 microfiche). Maps and drawings from the Dutch Colonial Archives in The Hague.

AMERICAN AUTOMOBILE ASSOCIATION COLLECTION (64 items). Printing plates illustrating the scribe printing technique.

AMERICAN COLONIZATION SOCIETY COLLECTION (22 folders). Maps of nineteenth-century Liberia by members of the American Colonization Society.

AMERICAN CONGRESS ON SURVEYING AND MAPPING (ACSM) AWARD MAPS (400 items). Maps submitted to the annual map design competition sponsored by the American Congress on Surveying and Mapping, 1975–1990.

AMERICAN MAP COLLECTION (167 items). Rare maps of North America printed between 1750 and 1790.

ASSOCIATION OF AMERICAN RAILROADS LIBRARY COLLECTION (91 folders). Printed railroad and transportation maps.

ATLANTIC NEPTUNE COLLECTION (1,369 items). Printed navigational charts of American coastal waters and harbors by Joseph Frederick Wallet Des Barres, 1774–1794.

ATLAS DUST COVERS (125 items). Dust covers from atlases, 1834–present.

NATHANIEL PRENTISS BANKS COLLECTION (22 items). Civil War maps relating to operations conducted by General Banks, Commander of the Department of the Gulf.

JOHN BARRETT COLLECTION (85 items). Maps of Latin American and Asia acquired by the American diplomat and director of the Pan American Union, 1894–1920.

J. NEILSON BARRY COLLECTION (138 items dispersed in the collections). Manuscript maps and tracings prepared by Barry relating to his study of the exploration of the Pacific northwest.

CLARA BARTON PAPERS (36 items). Maps of Europe and the United States collected by Barton, 1877–1903.

H. BENNETT COLLECTION (1,000 items). Fire insurance maps of small towns in Iowa, 1890–1910.

ANDREW H. BENTON-HERSCHEL V. JONES COLLECTION (4,706 items dispersed in the collections). Maps, atlas sheets, printed title pages, time lines, topographic profiles, and fortification plans, 1541–1915.

JOHN BIGELOW COLLECTION (359 items dispersed in the collections). Atlases, manuscript tracings, photocopies, and printed maps of the Columbian discoveries and the Isthmuses of Panama and Suez.

WILLIAM BINGHAM ESTATE MAPS (23 items). Manuscript land ownership atlases and maps of property in Maine, New York, and Pennsylvania, 1790s–1872.

TASKER HOWARD BLISS PAPERS (179 items). Maps pertaining to World War I and the Paris Peace Conference.

BRAILLE MAPS (130 items dispersed in the division's collections). Examples of maps devised for the blind and visually handicapped, 1936–1985.

BRITTLE BOOK MAPS COLLECTION (680 folders). Printed maps removed from books and serials from the general collections.

CARTOON MAPS COLLECTION (20 items). Manuscript drawings prepared for the *Chicago Tribune*, *Saturday Evening Post*, *Time*, and *Liberty*, 1928–1940s.

CLOTH MAP COLLECTION (400 items). Maps printed or photoreproduced on various fibers such as silk and tissue, 1626–1987.

COMMERCIAL DECAL COMPANY, INCORPORATED (192 folders). Maps printed for the U.S. Army Map Service, 1943–1945.

COPELAND RAILROAD SURVEYS COLLECTION (364 items). Maps and timetables for railroads in the United States showing freight traffic density, 1921–1953.

COPYRIGHT MAP TITLES COLLECTION (600 items). Map titles deposited with U.S. District Courts, 1790–1896.

ROBERT CROZIER COLLECTION (35 items). Maps, photomaps, and aerial photographs prepared by the 654th Engineering Topographical Battalion in France and Germany, 1944–1945.

THE CUMBERLAND MAP COLLECTION (666 microfiche). Military campaign maps from the Duke of Cumberland archives, eighteenth–nineteenth centuries.

WILLIAM MORRIS DAVIS DRAWINGS (71 items). Manuscript physiographic sketches and block diagrams illustrating the cycle of erosion, 1930s.

JOHN DISTURNELL COLLECTION (27 maps). Printed and photocopy maps of twenty-four editions of Disturnell's map of Mexico, 1826–1858.

EARTH OBSERVATION SATELLITE COMPANY (EOSAT) COLLECTION (120 items). Large format Landsat photographic images of selected features of the Earth, 1980s.

MELVILLE EASTHAM COLLECTION (444 items). Rare atlases and maps printed in Europe, 1571–circa 1850.

ENVIRONMENTAL SYSTEMS RESEARCH INSTITUTE, INCORPORATED (ESRI) COLLECTION (2,000 items). Innovative computer-generated maps exhibited at the annual ESRI Users' Conference from 1988–1993.

ENVIRONMENTAL SYSTEMS RESEARCH INSTITUTE, INCORPORATED (ESRI) MAP FILES (19 computer disks). Electronic files containing cartographic and statistical data for United States and world.

WILLIAM FADEN COLLECTION (101 items). Manuscript maps and plans of the French and Indian War and the American Revolution assembled by Faden, geographer to King George III, 1750s–1780s.

ETHEL M. FAIR COLLECTION (879 items). Pictorial maps from magazines, newspapers, and commercial printers, twentieth century.

MILLARD FILLMORE COLLECTION (247 items). Printed and manuscript maps of the United States and Europe collected by President Fillmore.

PETER FORCE COLLECTION (768 items). Manuscript and rare printed maps relating chiefly to the French and Indian War, the American Revolution, and the District of Columbia, 1685–1842.

THADDEUS M. FOWLER COLLECTION (224 items dispersed in the collections). Panoramic maps of American cities prepared by Fowler, 1881–1922.

GAMES AND PUZZLES (110 items). Representative examples of maps designed to serve as games and educational aids, 1822–1980s.

JEREMY FRANCIS GILMAN COLLECTION (75 items dispersed in collection). Photostatic copies of Confederate Civil War maps from originals at the U.S. Military Academy at West Point, Virginia Historical Society, and College of William and Mary.

GLOBE COLLECTION (450 items dispersed in collection). Original and facsimile terrestrial and celestial globes and globe gores, 1543–1990s.

CHARLES E. GOAD COMPANY COLLECTION (3,900 items). Fire insurance maps for 1,300 towns and cities in Canada, 1891–1973.

THE H. M. GOUSHA COMPANY COLLECTION (30 items). Painted zinc map plates created by Hal Shelton for the Jeppesen Company, 1950s–1960s.

JANET GREEN COLLECTION (636 items). Atlases, atlas title pages, globes, reference books.

GENERAL PETER H. HAGNER COLLECTION (40 items dispersed in the collections). Maps and sketches relating to Mexico, 1771–1840s.

RICHARD EDES HARRISON DRAWINGS (243 items). Manuscript sketch maps and final drawings prepared by Harrison for *Fortune, Time, Life,* and major map publishers, 1930s–1970s.

HENRY HARRISSE COLLECTION (615 items). Manuscript charts of the exploration of North America, 1606–1650, and Harrisse's study collection of facsimiles relating to the exploration of America.

KARL M. HAUSHOFER COLLECTION (21 maps). Printed topographic maps of Germany and Austria collected by Haushofer, a leading exponent of German geopolitics, 1930s.

HAUSLAB-LIECHTENSTEIN COLLECTION (10,000 items). Manuscript and printed military, topographic, and thematic maps assembled by the Austrian cartographer Franz Ritter von Hauslab and later acquired by Prince Johann II of Liechtenstein, nineteenth century.

EDWARD EVERETT HAYDEN AND FAMILY PAPERS (85 items). Maps and charts relating to Hayden's naval service as a marine meteorologist, 1880s–1920.

SAMUEL P. HEINTZELMANN PAPERS (20 items). Manuscript and printed maps relating to the Civil War and American southwest, 1839–1865.

ERNEST HEXAMER COLLECTION (5,000 items). Fire insurance maps of Philadelphia, 1857–1916.

JOHN HILLS COLLECTION (20 maps). Manuscript maps prepared for Sir Henry Clinton by Hills relating to British military operations in New Jersey, 1778–1781.

GENERAL JOHN L. HINES COLLECTION (187 maps). Annotated maps of American military activities in France during World War I.

JEDEDIAH HOTCHKISS MAPS AND FIELD NOTES (600 items). Prepared by the Confederate surveyor during the Civil War.

RICHARD HOWE COLLECTION (72 items). Nautical charts used by Adm. Lord Richard Howe, Commander in Chief of British Fleet, 1750s–1770s.

ARTHUR W. HUMMEL COLLECTION (85 items). Scrolls, wall maps, and atlases of China donated by Andrew W. Mellon and Hummel, Ming period (1368–1644)–1912.

ANDREW JACKSON COLLECTION (11 items). Manuscript maps associated with General Jackson's campaigns during the War of 1812.

JAPANESE ARMY ROUTE MAPS (397 items). Manuscript route maps of Korea and China prepared by Japanese military engineers, 1878–1880s.

THOMAS JEFFERSON COLLECTION (30 items). Reproductions of maps, field notes, and plans from the Papers of Thomas Jefferson, 1746–1825.

JOHN JOHNSON MAPS AND NOTEBOOKS (4 items). U.S.-Canadian boundary survey, 1817.

GEORGE KENNAN PAPERS (13 items). Printed maps of Russia, 1750–1940s.

JOHANN GEORG KOHL DRAWINGS (575 items). Manuscript copies by Kohl during the 1850s of maps in European collections relating to the discovery and exploration of North America.

MOKUSSI KUWAHARA LIBRARY (163 items dispersed in the collections). Printed and manuscript maps of Suruga Province, Japan, collected by Kuwahara for history of province.

JONATHAN T. LANMAN SLIDE COLLECTION (650 items). 35mm color slides of maps relating to European exploration and discovery and East Asia.

ROBERT LANSING COLLECTION (10 items). Atlases relating to the Alaska Boundary Tribune and North Atlantic Fishery Arbitration, 1895–1909.

WALDO G. LELAND COLLECTION. Inventory of maps of North America found in the Bibliotheque Nationale and the archives of the Service Hydrographique de la Marine, Paris.

LEWIS AND CLARK COLLECTION (20 items). Manuscript maps associated with William Clark, 1796–1832.

WOODBURY LOWERY COLLECTION (300 items). Study collection of original and facsimile maps relating to early Spanish exploration and settlement in North America.

MAGELLAN GEOGRAPHIX DATABASE (56 computer disks). Electronic map files providing worldwide coverage of selected places.

MAGGS CHART COLLECTION (369 items dispersed in the collection). Manuscript nautical charts, chiefly of South America, prepared by students at the Naval Academy in Cadiz, Spain, 1729–1824.

MATTHEW FONTAINE MAURY COLLECTION (160 items). Published wind and current charts by Maury, 1848–1850s.

GEORGE B. MCCLELLAN COLLECTION (27 maps). Sketch maps and fortification plans drawn or collected by McClellan as a cadet at West Point, 1842–1846, and maps of the Virginia Military District in Ohio.

SHANNON MCCUNE COLLECTION (22 items). Scrolls, atlases, woodblocks, and fan maps of Korea and Japan, fifteenth–nineteenth centuries.

WILLIAM MCKINLEY PAPERS (11 items). Printed maps of China and the United States.

JOHN MELISH COLLECTION (35 items). Series of engraved wall maps of the United States compiled and printed by Melish, 1816–1823.

MYLON MERRIAM COLLECTION (1,150 items). Topographic maps, city plans, oblique images and panoramic views, chiefly of Switzerland, 1850–1950s.

MICROFILM COLLECTION (101 microfilm reels). Rare maps from archives, libraries, and mapping organizations in France, Great Britain, Italy, The Netherlands, Panama, Spain, and the United States, 1410–1924.

IRIS MILLER COLLECTION (600 items). Manuscript and printed maps, architectural drawings, and "charrettes" of Washington, D.C.

THEODORE MILLER DRAWINGS (4,786 items). Manuscript maps and atlases prepared by Miller for his *Graphic History of the Americas* and works in progress.

MINNESOTA AND DAKOTA FIRE UNDERWRITERS MAP COLLECTION (1,528 items). Fire insurance maps for small towns in Minnesota, North Dakota, and South Dakota, 1894–1970s.

MINTO COLLECTION (14 items dispersed in the collection). Manuscript maps of the Indonesian archipelago formerly in the possession of Gilbert Elliot, 1st Earl of Minto and Governor General of India, 1807–1814.

JOHN MITCHELL COLLECTION (32 maps). Various editions of Mitchell's Map of North America, 1755–1779.

NASA PRINT COLLECTION (630 items). Color photo images (8- by 10-inch) of the Earth generated from satellite sensing devices, 1972–1978.

NIERENSTEIN NATIONAL REALITY COMPANY (354 folders). Atlases, maps, and aerial photographs of American and Canadian cities and shopping centers, 1920s–1950s.

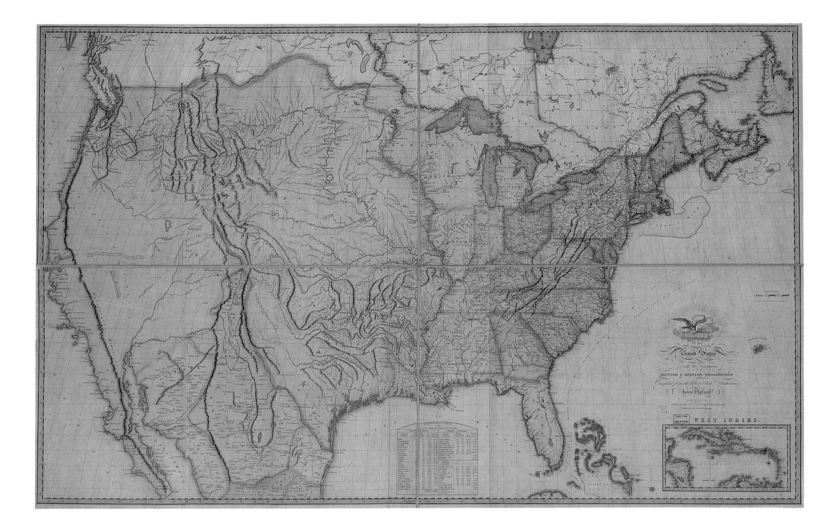

"Map of the United States with the contiguous British and Spanish Possessions" (Philadelphia, 1816). is the first wall map of the United States published by John Melish, the leading American map publisher of his day. The Geography and Map Division holds twenty-one of the twenty-five known states of this map. *(John Melish Collection)*

PIERRE OZANNE DRAWINGS (23 items). Maps of views of French naval engagements in the West Indies and North America by Ozanne, a marine artist with French naval forces, 1770s.

PANAMA CANAL ZONE LIBRARY-MUSEUM MAP COLLECTION (505 items). Manuscript and printed maps relating to the Panama Canal Zone, circa 1700–1967.

MURIEL H. PARRY COLLECTION (800 items). Pictorial maps, including a set of English shire maps by the noted illustrator, Ernest Clegg.

JOSEPH R. PASSONNEAU COLLECTION (26 items). Manuscript historic maps of Georgetown and Washington, D.C., by Passonneau and associates.

CHARLES OSCAR PAULLIN COLLECTION (62 portfolios). Maps relating to congressional voting patterns, 1791–1883, used in the preparation of his *Historical Atlas of the United States.*

ORLANDO M. POE COLLECTION (16 items). Civil War maps from the papers of General Poe.

PORTUGUESE-SPANISH BOUNDARY COMMISSION MAPS (29 items dispersed in the collections). Manuscript and photocopy surveys of the Brazil-Uruguay frontier, 1780s.

POWDER HORN COLLECTION (8 items). Powder horns with maps and views inscribed by soldiers, 1750s to 1812.

PRINTING TECHNOLOGY COLLECTION (15 items, dispersed in division's collections). Woodblocks, copperplates, lithographic stones, glass plates, and plastic separation sheets used for printing maps, 1682–1980s.

ERWIN RAISZ COLLECTION (96 items). Printed landform maps prepared by Raisz, 1939–1963.

CHARLES RASCHER COLLECTION (5,000 items). Fire insurance maps of Chicago, nineteenth century.

CHARLES RAU COLLECTION (20 items). Drawings by Rau showing cartographic techniques, 1841–1854.

REMOTE SENSING IMAGERY AND AERIAL PHOTOGRAPHY BROWSE FILE (25,000 items). Film cassettes and microfiche indexes of images of the Earth taken from satellites and aircraft, 1960s–1990s.

WALTER W. RISTOW CHRISTMAS CARD COLLECTION (500 items). Christmas cards illustrated with maps, globes, and cartographic instruments, 1940s–1980s.

ROCHAMBEAU COLLECTION (122 items). Maps and plans of military fortifications and troop positions in North America prepared for Jean Baptiste Donatien de Vimeur, compte de Rochambeau, commander of French forces, 1777–1783.

ADMIRAL JOHN RODGERS COLLECTION (92 items dispersed in the collections). Printed portolan charts of North America issued by the Spanish Dirección de Hidrografía, 1818.

THEODORE ROOSEVELT PAPERS (9 items). Manuscript and annotated maps pertaining principally to Russo-Japanese War, 1905.

LESSING J. ROSENWALD GIFT (11 items dispersed in the collection). Rare printed maps and atlases, 1562–eighteenth century.

MARCIAN F. ROSSI COLLECTION (279 items). Vellum maps of the known world attributed to the era of Marco Polo and supporting materials.

ALBERT RUGER COLLECTION (198 items). Panoramic views of midwestern cities published by Ruger, 1860s–1870s.

RUSSIAN PALACES LIBRARY COLLECTION (170 items). Printed maps, principally of Russia, from four palace libraries in Czarist Russia, 1827–1858.

SANBORN FIRE INSURANCE COMPANY COLLECTION (700,000 items). Detailed maps of 12,000 American cities and towns, 1867–1980s.

WILLIAM TECUMSEH SHERMAN COLLECTION (205 items). Maps and atlases relating to Sherman's military campaigns during the Civil War.

GUY-HAROLD SMITH DRAWINGS (15 items dispersed in the collections). Manuscript drawings of physiographic diagrams of South America and western states, 1930s.

ALBERT SPEER MATERIALS (28 items). Maps and plans of the redevelopment of Berlin prepared for Adolf Hitler, 1933–1942.

EPHRAIM GEORGE SQUIER COLLECTION (38 maps). Manuscript and printed maps of Central America relating to canals and railroads, 1850s–1880s.

CHARLES PELOT SUMMERALL PAPERS (363 items dispersed in the collections). Personal collection of manuscript, annotated, and printed World War I battle maps of General Summerall.

HERBERT THATCHER BEQUEST (76 items dispersed in the collections). Ptolemaic atlases and manuscript tracings of maps of North America, nineteenth century.

GILBERT THOMPSON COLLECTION (134 items). Maps, photographs, and topographic views relating to western exploration, 1850s–1896.

THREE-DIMENSIONAL RAISED RELIEF MAPS (2,300 items). Three-dimensional raised relief maps and terrain models printed or painted on plaster, papier-mâché, vinyl plastic, or sponge rubber, 1879–1990s.

EDGAR TOBIN AERIAL SURVEYS COLLECTION. (240 items). Aerial photographic mosaic prints of southern states, 1953–1954.

JOSEPH MEREDITH TONER COLLECTION (32 items). Manuscript maps and tracings relating to Washington, D.C., 1790s–1880s.

TWENTY-SEVENTH INTERNATIONAL GEOGRAPHICAL CONGRESS MAP EXHIBITION (1,962 items dispersed in the collections). Atlases, maps, aerial photographs, remote sensing images, and cartography and geography books from thirty-seven countries, 1992.

UNITED KINGDOM INTER-SERVICE TOPOGRAPHICAL DEPARTMENT COLLECTION (200 volumes). Topographic intelligence reports containing maps, terrain descriptions, and aerial photographs of military sites in Europe and Southeast Asia during World War II.

U.S. CENSUS BUREAU MAPS (803 folders). Block statistics maps for standard metropolitan areas, 1980 and 1990.

U.S. CENSUS BUREAU TIGER/LINE FILES (47 computer discs). Electronic data base for 1990 decennial map of the United States.

U.S. COAST AND GEODETIC SURVEY LIBRARY (207 items). Manuscript and printed nautical charts of the Great Lakes and coastal regions of the United States, 1830–1968.

U.S. CONGRESSIONAL SERIAL SET (17,000 items). Maps published by Congress as enclosures in Congressional publications, 1817–1909.

U.S. DEFENSE MAPPING AGENCY DATA FILES (6 computer disks). Digital chart of the world.

U.S. GEOLOGICAL SURVEY DATA FILES (20 computer disks). Electronic spatial data relating to a variety of scientific programs.

U.S. GEOLOGICAL SURVEY REPORTS (13,600 folders). Geologic and hydrologic maps from scientific reports.

U.S. NATIONAL CANCER INSTITUTE MAPPING PROGRAM (16 computer disks). Electronic maps of cancer mortality by county.

U.S. OFFICE OF STRATEGIC SERVICES (OSS) MAP COLLECTION (1,300 items dispersed in the collections). General and thematic maps produced by OSS during World War II.

U.S. OFFICE OF STRATEGIC SERVICES (OSS) MICROFILM COLLECTION (101 microfilm reels). Maps from various libraries in the United States filmed during World War II.

VAULT MAP COLLECTION (3,000 items). Manuscript and printed maps maintained separately for their unique, artistic, or historical significance, sixteenth–twentieth centuries.

VELLUM CHART COLLECTION (33 items). Rare nautical atlases and charts on vellum, 1484–seventeenth century.

LANGDON WARNER COLLECTION (30 items). Manuscript maps, atlases, and fan maps of Korea and China collected by Warner, director of the first and second China expeditions of the Fogg Museum, Harvard University, Ming Dynasty–nineteenth century.

GEORGE WASHINGTON ATLAS SOURCE MATERIALS COLLECTIONS (1,308 items). Chiefly photocopies of maps and text used by Lawrence Martin in the production of the *George Washington Atlas* (1932).

GEORGE WASHINGTON MAPS (12 items dispersed in collection). Manuscript and published plans and plats drawn by George Washington and his associates, 1749–1793.

WASHINGTON METROPOLITAN AREA TRANSIT AUTHORITY (METRO) MAPS (33 items). Translucent maps of the Washington, D.C., METRO system.

MARY J. WEBB COLLECTION (39 items). Tracings of nineteenth-century maps of Texas relating to early land grants.

HOWARD WELSH COLLECTION (29 items). Globes and maps published in the United States during the nineteenth century.

ALPHONSO WHIPPLE COLLECTION (2,000 items). Fire insurance maps of St. Louis, nineteenth century.

CAPTAIN JAMES M. WILLIS COLLECTION (15 items). Manuscript nautical charts, drawing and writing instruments, and chart case belonging to Willis, 1852–1875.

WOODROW WILSON PAPERS (8 maps). Manuscript and printed political boundary maps prepared primarily for the Paris Peace Conference, 1918–1919.

YUDIN COLLECTION (6 items). Archaeological maps and maps of gold-mining concessions in Yiniseysk District, Russia, 1858–1900.